The Other Side of Cancer

Living Life with My Dying Sister

Annette Leeds

Dedication

To Doctor Harms, a wonderful doctor who stood by my sister's side and helped her carry the burden of her cancer. Never giving her false hope, but rather encouraging her to do the things she wanted to do before she died. It was your selfless, kindhearted, and unwavering dedication that gave her peace. You spent those difficult months with us empowering our family with your wisdom and strength. Your commitment to her never dwindled, allowing her to feel safe until it was time for her to go.

Introduction

In January 2016, an unbiased cancer took my sister, Theresa, from me. Memories are all I have now; some are so painful to recall, while others bring me tremendous laughter. Even though I know she isn't physically with me anymore, when I think of my sister, I feel her presence so deep within my heart. Whether it is a chill running through me, or a warm, loving feeling, I can only hope it is Theresa, and not my imagination getting the best of me.

The crystal vase she loved so much is now where her ashes rest. As I pass the open door of her room, there is no longer any sign of her; just an empty room she used to call home. I try to find comfort from my sorrow by lying on the floor in her room, staring up at the ceiling, hoping she will send me some sign that she is okay.

There are those days when I think I won't be able to get through another day without her, avoiding those closest to me, angry with myself that I couldn't save her. Each day, it is difficult to wake up without some thought of her, and with the burning question: Why was she taken from me? I long for a time when the sadness subsides, but with that comes the reality that she is no longer here ... making our family incomplete.

We went through life protecting each other from harm, and, when she needed it the most, I was unable to protect her from this callous creature we call cancer. I will no longer have my sister, with whom I shared so many great times. The inside stories that only she and I understood have vanished, leaving me without my partner-in-crime.

Using my journal as a shield from the pain, I documented our time together, knowing when she was gone I had captured her last months in black and white. She showed me the meaning of bravery and strength. Her days were not empty. She embraced life and lived it while dying. There were so many times I was truly amazed at how gracefully she accepted what lie ahead for her, as if someone let her in on that big secret we all wonder about: Where do we go when we leave here?

She always believed that if your dreams didn't scare you, they weren't big enough. I know she is watching and smiling, helping me through my heartache with her infectious laughter and unwavering courage.

Chapter 1

"It all began fifty-five years ago with a smack to the butt. It is that smack that started me down a road of independence, strong will, and an unwavering love of humor. Laughter is my peace.
"I've been loved by the right people and crushed by the wrong. It is those lessons I've learned that made me who I am today."
— From Theresa's Journal

Each family in the neighborhood had its own signature beckoning method for calling their children for supper. Whether it was a harsh whistle from Mr. Caine or the chuck wagon triangle from Mrs. Yen, kids scattered through the streets, running to their perspective houses when their signature sound rang out. Ours was the cowbell. Whether you were down the street at a friend's, doing homework, or hiding in your room to avoid your chores, when the loud clang of the bell plowed through the neighborhood, you had better be at the dinner table.

Gathering six kids, along with Mom and Dad, made for unpredictable situations with all of us assembled at the dinner table. Inevitably, one of us was always late, which met the wrath of my mom. I remember one time I came home late and she stood on a step stool by the back door and jumped out at me like Cato from the *Pink Panther*, spanking me with a tennis shoe in front of everyone. Not one of them warned me but rather viewed it as pre-dinner entertainment.

Raised in a staunch Catholic family, my eldest brother led us in prayer to say grace, blessing the food as if he were speaking at an important public event. He always seemed to make it an elaborate recitation, as if auditioning for a part in a play. We held hands until he reached the finale, "Amen," and that is when the antics began.

There was no fooling around or excessive talking allowed. Instead, we exchanged private jokes between us with either eye contact or a swift kick under the table. Mom would glare at each of us, hoping to keep us all in line. Then, the same stern warning would emerge from her. "Eat, and stop all the tee-heeing," she insisted.

Each night at the dinner table seemed to provide us with a new tale. Whether it was vegetable night and my sister, Sophie, storing them in her cheeks like a chipmunk, waiting to make a break for the bathroom to either flush them down the toilet, which would, eventually, turn back up, or chucking them out my eldest sister's, Margaret's, window into the neighbor's trash cans. Either way, dinner was like an Olympic event.

Theresa, too young and too small to pull off any of the stunts, the older siblings always wangled her into taking the blame for them, and she welcomed the mission without hesitation. Over and over, they uttered the same words…

"Tell Dad you did it," they insisted. "He won't spank you."

No fool to the capers of the eldest, Dad would spank everyone, no matter what. He figured if you did nothing wrong that time, you must have done something else of which he was unaware.

My brother, James, would raise his hand as if he were winning something. "I'll go first," he proclaimed.

Margaret, our mother hen, would cry a steady stream of tears for each of us as we took our punishment. Dad would hold us by one arm and give us a stern spanking. Our bodies, acting like pendulums, would swing back into his space, allowing him to give the second swat.

Night after night, Mom and Dad repeated the same dinner scenario, trying to get six, independent children to eat what they believed was a "wholesome meal" in front of them, only to have it met with rejection and rebellion.

Margaret would sit for what seemed like an eternity, picking her food apart, looking for pieces of fat she was sure were hiding on her plate. Often, we could hear her boyfriend in the far distance of the house, chucking rocks at her bedroom window so they could canoodle after curfew.

Sophie had an assigned place at the table next to my dad. I marveled at her conviction, holding her ground against eating anything resembling a vegetable. He would force her to eat each bite and watch her as she swallowed. Sophie spent many nights sitting on the hearth of the fireplace to finish her dinner, well after the rest of us finished eating. Dad would hold a vigil on a chair next to the fireplace, giving him a clear view of her, forcing her to eat each bite until her plate was clean.

"You're not leaving that fireplace until all that food is gone," he insisted.

Sophie never responded with words. Her stuffed cheeks and stern glare revealing her stubbornness spoke volumes. Hunger never seemed to win; she would rather starve than eat what was in front of her.

The night forged on for hours until she emptied her plate. I was never sure where the food went, but I know she didn't eat it. I thought if they ever sold that house someday, the new owners would, for sure, find lumps of petrified food stuffed in the fireplace chute.

In contrast to her siblings, Phyllis behaved most nights, until it came time to clean up. She was like an undercover spy. We were careful to place discarded food in our napkins, and she oversaw disposing of the evidence without notice.

I, the youngest child, sat close to Mom. Being the baby awarded me special treatment of not having to eat most of the concoctions laid out in front of us. The tense negotiation of "just take one more bite" occurred each evening. Mom would push a small portion toward me, motioning me to eat a little bit, and then taking the rest from my plate.

James, however, was our human garbage disposal, eating anything and everything, including our leftovers, without hesitation. Like a beanpole, he stood six feet tall and maybe weighed one hundred fifty pounds on a good day; always eating a constant stream of food to fill his never-ending hunger. He was an incredible athlete, consuming massive amounts of food most days as if he were heading to the electric chair.

Mom grocery shopped once a week. She would buy everything from breakfast to dinner, with some treats for the evening. On the day she would come home from the store, the milk would disappear and all the cookies would vanish, except for the crumbs, which one could access with a licked finger running across the bottom of the bag.

Mom had some doozy dinners that even made her and Dad cringe. Most notable was the lack of seasoning that might have provided some kind of taste. Often, she would cook the life out of most foods—meat, in particular. She would panfry and cook meat until a hard, charcoal crust covered the once-pink surface. On occasion, she would break out some Belgium family tradition, resembling something you would feed prisoners of war. Masters at the craft of disguising their emotions, Mom and Dad played off the dreadful dishes. I remember an eggplant incident. She insisted the slimy, bitter, lifeless brown gush that sat on each of our plates was healthy for us. We all stared at her, waiting for *her* to take the first bite. She slipped a small piece off her fork and into her mouth. Then, without hesitation, she pushed herself back from the table.

"You don't have to eat it," she insisted. "It must be spoiled."

We glanced at each other with smirks, excited she spared us the dreadful creation. That night, we had Kentucky Fried Chicken.

Our favorite meal, which came around occasionally, was Italian food. Dad is Sicilian and from a very large Italian family. In his house, spaghetti sauce from a jar was a sin. Therefore, my grandmother taught Mom how to make the best sauce and meatballs you could ever imagine, surely able to compete with anyone's *Nona*. Those nights were probably the only time we were "dysfunctional" at the dinner table, with all of us squeezed shoulder-to-shoulder, passing food around in rapid succession as if it were our last meal.

I remember one night that gave us years of overwhelming laughter. Theresa was always the most innocent at dinner, yet quite clumsy, which usually involved her knocking over her glass of milk, forcing everyone to frantically push away from our places, hoping not to get wet.

That evening, as usual, the plate of meatballs at the table had been wiped clean. Dad asked Theresa to get him another meatball from the large brewing pot in the kitchen. Without hesitation, she jumped from her chair and headed to the kitchen. She poked her head back into the dining room and uttered, "Extra sauce, too?"

He nodded.

A short time later, she emerged, bobbling the plate in one hand and holding a napkin in the other. Stepping down into the dining room, she tripped. All I heard behind me was, "Whoops!" A sound like hail hitting a window came next. We all turned to view the saucy meatball sailing through the air as it bounced harshly against the popcorn ceiling, dropping to the floor, and continuing its journey across the carpet, coming to an abrupt halt—sauceless and resting next to Dad's foot. Silence hovered, as we were unsure what was to come next. As the unexpected grin came over his face, we knew his guard was down, something that didn't happen often. We all chuckled to ourselves, as she gingerly reached for the meatball.

"Let me get you another one," she demanded. "This one has lint on it."

As time passed, attendance at dinner began to diminish. All the funny stories were now just memories we spoke about on special occasions or at gatherings. The eldest siblings had moved on with their now-adult lives, whether it was off to the service for my brother or getting married for my sisters, making Theresa and me the last to remain at home with Mom and Dad.

Eventually, the time came for Theresa to move on, too. At a young age, she seemed far more driven than the rest of us kids. She used to read all sorts of books for hours at a time. I am not a person who likes to read, so it seemed more like a punishment than a pleasure.

Being close in age, we shared even more great times the other kids weren't around for—the secret stories and inside jokes that only the two of us understood. When we got together as a family, we would play games. Of course, she and I were partners, always beating our elders without much effort.

"You two are such cheaters," they balked.

That was the furthest from the truth; we just had a bond none of them experienced. Almost like we could read each other's minds or something.

Like with her reading, she was dedicated and ambitious. She moved out at seventeen years old and into her own apartment, never looking back. Even though I felt abandoned when she left me, I knew she was destined for great things. It showed in every ounce of her being. The determination she projected was something I have never seen from any other person in my life. As she got older, her fortitude never wavered.

Chapter 2

Like most hardworking people, you look forward to the occasional vacation that allows you to do the things you love most. For my sister, it was letting the ocean *swoosh* across her feet as the sand buried her toes. Swimming with the sea turtles in Maui was more meaningful and gave her the most peace. She finally could relax and enjoy the fruits of all her many years of hard work and sacrifice. She wanted to eat good food and live the dream life she worked so hard to achieve.

Only a few months earlier, Theresa had finally begun feeling the effects of success. Notoriety at work for all the long, painstaking hours and sleepless nights that drove her to the top of her career were finally coming to fruition.

Her hopes and dreams did not sway her body, though. All the risks and the unrelenting time she spent working to better her life for herself and her children would, once again, seem out of reach. Her health began to fail, forcing her to face an adversary she never counted on.

This time, her coping mechanism couldn't fix the problem by looking past it for the next strategic move. All through her life, she was able to survive difficult situations by reviewing what was in front of her, sidestepping the problem, and focusing on a better solution.

She began experiencing what she described as heart-pounding chest pains, followed by what seemed like the horrendous flu. Unable to keep up with the voracious symptoms tormenting her, she had a worker from her office drive her to the local hospital. The symptoms were so severe she recalled barely being able to catch her breath.

Chalked up to being overworked and dehydrated, she came home with a barf bag for comfort. It was the eve of Thanksgiving, as she sat alone in a wheelchair at the emergency room entrance, waiting for her roommate to give her a ride home.

She went over the symptoms many times in her head. In hindsight, the relentless back pain and abrupt weight loss should have seemed obvious to her that it was some type of cancer. Yet, her grueling schedule and long hours convinced her to believe she was just overloaded and fatigued from her long days. As the month passed, she managed to get nausea and weight loss under control with a constant flow of antacids. Although that was short-lived, as endless trips to the emergency room replaced time that could have spent with family during the holidays.

She became increasingly lethargic from nauseousness and vomiting. Still weak and unable to return to work, she went to see a general surgeon for severe stomach pains. They ran several tests and decided her gallbladder could possibly be the culprit. The surgeon removed it prophylactically, which seemed to give her some relief.

Beset by professional and financial demands, she returned to work. Desperate not to lose ground at her job, she jumped back into her grueling schedule. Her son, Christopher, was away at college, and the need to keep that dream alive for him drove her to plow forward. Still, her progressing health concerns were demanding as well, leaving her in pain and overwhelmingly weak. She tried to go through the motions, but her body was taking charge.

She was at the peak of her career, as a well-respected chief financial officer of a large hospital. She had struggled through the most rigorous times and demanding hours. Hadn't her body realized she had made it to the top? Receiving jobs offers from all over the country, she had the pick of her professional future.

With her dream job and limitless personal prospects, the enticing possibilities were endless. She had written her own version of the American dream, succeeding in a male-driven world, while continuing to remain true to her own self.

She single-handedly made herself into a powerhouse. Growing up, she thought being skinny was the key to life. She was plump and plain, but as her success grew, thin thighs no longer measured her triumphs. Her accomplishments gave her far more than a perfect body; it gave her accolades that most would envy. This, however, did not come without sacrifice and friction from those closest to her.

As kids, Mom and Dad raised us to believe life was not complete without a husband and children. She married a man ten years her senior, desperate to achieve the fairy-tale life she learned to believe in. She would soon complete the circle of life by having two children with him. A few years into their marriage, her husband lost his job, forcing her to support their household. In the months following, he never regained control of their family. She continued to be the sole supporter; slaving away to support their family, yet not seemed bothered by it.

His lack of employment drove a wedge in their relationship. She grew fiercer and more assertive, and he viewed her professional achievements as an unfortunate "mocking" of his inability to take care of their family. The balance of power had shifted, leaving him devastated.

She realized the buck stopped with her. She became increasingly more ambitious about her career and taking care of her family. Instead of her husband embracing his determined wife, he became distant and resentful of her, feeling dejected as a husband and father. This became a pivotal point, and their relationship spiraled downward, ultimately ending in divorce.

As a young woman living alone and having to support her family from a distance, she faced difficult times. The narrative she had to embrace was going it alone and leaving her children to live with her now ex-husband. Now, more than ever, having to climb out of her financial hardship and turn her life—and those counting on her—into a positive, her career life turned into an ebb and flow of tremendous achievements and agonizing failures. I'm not sure if she worked so hard to get where she was for herself, or to prove the naysayers wrong.

Soon, she would meet and marry a man she thought would change her life, share in her victories, and help her through the difficult times. However, he took her success and determination as a vehicle to quit his job and live off of her. Floundering between jobs and running up credit card debt as if they had the money to support his extravagant lifestyle now gave her yet *another* hurdle to overcome. She suddenly became his parent, scolding him for excessive spending and lack of respect for all her hard work. Their relationship turned into an asexual arrangement. He acted like a child, and, therefore, she became his mother.

Subsequently, cheated on her with several women, while she struggled to keep her head above water, which was far more than she was willing to accept. Once again, the ugly heartbreaking reality reared its ugly head; the men she chose relied on her being more capable and driven only to further their own lives. This husband drove her deeper and deeper into debt. Teetering on the edge of being homeless and in personal and financial ruin, she kept her head down and plowed through her hardships, working longer hours, continually searching for that one break. Her fortitude, perhaps, was driving her straight into the ground.

When she finally decided to dig herself out from the wreckage of two failed marriages and a mountain of debt, it became a humbling experience. Her first step was to lose a whopping two hundred sixty-five pounds—that second husband—who was sucking the last bit of financial and emotional life out of her.

After spending the last fifteen years in failing relationships, she vowed she would never fool herself into thinking a man was the answer to all her hopes and dreams. The idea of sharing a life with a partner did not appear to be in her future anytime soon. She tried to live the life she was raised to believe was the right path, but she was unsuccessful. From that day forward, she promised herself she would live the life she dreamed of and not anyone else's version.

Failure at work was no longer an option. Over the next few years, it became her mission to climb the corporate ladder quickly and efficiently. She refused to take "no" for an answer. Plowing through impervious obstacles, she challenged the double standard that awarded men positions over women.

As she gained strength and success in her career, she became an advancing executive. Wealth and achievements were the driving force behind her obsession to stay on top, both in her personal and professional life. Pathologically paranoid of financial hardship, she worked long hours and made painstaking sacrifices to keep herself and her children in a lifestyle of which she long fantasized.

The one thing I think she never could get past was the constant reminder of her first marriage. While she turned herself into the breadwinner, she cringed at the remarks that her ex-husband was somehow a "saint" for taking care of their kids; something she would have gladly done had *he* supported their household.

What came next was something she never counted on. Her children were now growing into young adults. She spent as much time as she possibly could with them, whether in person or daily telephone calls. Her ex-husband allowed the children far too much freedom, and they began to stray to peers who were bad influences. Initially, she was emotionally numb at the thought of losing her relationship with her children, followed by rage. She was devastated. In the months following their absence, she spent her days encased in her work. She worked hard to give them the best life she knew, and yet, they punished her for that very thing. Her desire for vengeance turned into strength. She could only hope that someday they would realize she worked so hard for them and their futures.

I think her daughter's a new boyfriend, Clark, brought on her position. He had come from a colorful family background, riddled with drug abuse and alcoholism. Veronica was at a vulnerable time in her life, which allowed him to instill major abandonment issues about her mother. Compounding the problem, her father was afraid of Clark with his loud mouth and raging temper. Therefore, he didn't attempt to quash the relationship.

Her son, Christopher, on the other hand, was a teenager missing his mom. He seemed to go along with Veronica and the notion their mother left them to find a better life for herself, not realizing the need to support them brought on her absence.

During the estrangement from her mother, Veronica went through some difficult times. Trying to be the surrogate mother to Christopher, loyal daughter to her father, and now juggling a demonstrative boyfriend, her insecurities seemed to mirror that of her mother as a young girl, something of which Theresa was all too aware. Veronica, in the past, tried hard to be that strong woman her mom wanted her to be. However, I think Clark provided a path of least resistance to the woman she was not mentally capable of being.

Now, Veronica had found herself in an abusive situation, of which Theresa would eventually have to take control. Determined to repair her fractured relationship with her children, she asked if they wanted to come to live with her, but they were comfortable where they were. I think, somehow, they felt sorry for their father. She wanted to instill self-confidence in both her children, hoping to empower them to strive for the best in life. Christopher was very receptive, hoping to go to college in the fall. Veronica, however, fought the idea of college and the wisdom and empowerment that would come with a good education.

Although she kept away from Clark for some time, Veronica's self-doubt got the best of her, and she went right back to him. This was like a thorn in Theresa's side, that she somehow failed her daughter. She never condemned Veronica for going back with him, but rather tried to show her there was a better way. Unlike her mother, Veronica was not a fearsome person and chose to continue her relationship with him.

Theresa had been somewhat distant from Mom and Dad for some time. There had been a rift between her and Dad. Mom stood by him and, therefore, Theresa was absent for most of the family gatherings at their home. Because she lived so far away and her crazy schedule didn't give her much free time, I hadn't seen her in months.

Over time, the basis for their disagreement seemed inconsequential, and eventually, they mended fences. Rather than resolving the issue, they pushed it under the rug for the sake of the family.

Over the next few years, her life was a mystery to most of us. We were unaware of how successful and highly regarded Theresa had become in her field. Known for her larger-than-life stories when she was younger, always feeling the need to make any situation seem grander than it was, she didn't need to do that any longer. She had made it. She was living that impressive story she always talked about. Yet, it seemed no matter how triumphant and accomplished she became, she still felt unconvinced it was enough.

Chapter 3

As the week progressed, I received a telephone call from Mom, asking if I had seen Theresa. The week prior, Theresa made a call to Mom, telling her she was very sick. Instead of getting the comfort and support she was hoping for, Mom dismissed her feelings, thinking Theresa was just overreacting. Looking back, I think Theresa knew she was gravely ill and wanted some reassurance from her mother that she would be okay.

The holidays had passed, and I had forgotten about what had happened between Theresa and Mom. It was a late January evening. We were having some unseasonably warm weather, so I sat outside taking in the night, stars sparkling and the moon in full glow. Then, I received a telephone call from my sister, Margaret, telling me Theresa was in the hospital for observation. Geographically distant from all her loved ones, she drove herself to the hospital. Doubled over in pain, jaundice, and faced with irrepressible itching, she couldn't ignore the obvious signs of a serious illness. Her bilirubin had skyrocketed, causing the glowing yellow tone on her skin. We would later find out that she had a mass obstructing her common bile duct, which is responsible for transporting bile from the liver to the intestines. At that moment, the seriousness of her condition became real. The suffocating weight of what was happening was now tangible.

The hospital was close to Margaret's house, so she headed over to see if she could help or get some information on her condition. It was difficult to get any real straight answers from Theresa regarding her illness, refusing to allow any information released to anyone but herself. Over the last few years, I think she was feeling rejected by all of us because of the tension with Mom and Dad, so it only seemed natural she would hold her condition close to her heart.

As kids, we always took care of one another. Margaret tried to be supportive and break the barrier, but Theresa remained guarded. Margaret stayed at the hospital with her for several hours, trying to get some sense of what was wrong with her little sister.

Theresa's life, thus far, had taught her to be tough. Yet, I know her big sister gave her that ability to pause and let down the wall of distrust. She knew any distance felt between all of us would soon vanish if she could allow herself to let us in her life again.

Although Theresa had a tough exterior, inside she was fragile in many ways. When we were kids, she and I shared a room. I strategically slept furthest from the door, fearing if anyone tried to get us, they would nab her first. Petrified of the dark, I would run from the doorway and pounce on my bed across the room, leaving the overhead light glaring above our heads.

She would admonish me night after night. "Turn the light off. You were the last one in bed!"

I always had the same response. "I can sleep with the light on." One, because I was terrified of the dark, and two, I would do anything to annoy her. Deep down, I knew she, too, was afraid of the dark, which became more and more prevalent when she got sick.

Veronica felt it was necessary to call Theresa's second husband, Derek. Theresa began speaking to him again over the last year, but their relationship remained strained from his infidelities, and she had moved on to a new life. She was over it, and she was unwilling to subject herself to his incessant begging to take him back. She was empty inside; no pleading was going to bring her back. Besides, their renewed relationship was still toxic, which caused such an emotional uproar most times.

The precise nature of her condition remained unclear for the next few days, but it didn't look promising; clearly, there was an obstruction. Doctors attempted another biopsy, but, once again, failure won. They placed a drain to relieve the pressure from whatever was causing the blockage. Tethered to an IV pole, she was on fluids and she was beginning to feel better without the pressure from the poisonous bile building up in her body. For the first time, instead of resistance and heartbreak from outsiders, her own body was betraying her.

Too sick to take care of herself, she stayed with Veronica, Clark, and her first husband, John. Still unwilling to let her siblings step up, she decided to move in with them strictly out of desperation. Painfully real, though, was the demand for monetary restitution. Even in her critical condition, she felt pressured to provide financial support.

Most women wouldn't anticipate having to move back in with their ex-husband, but that is where her daughter lived and she seemed to have no alternative plan. I truly believe John never stopped loving her. She was his true love, so I think insecurities and heartbreak brought on most of his actions when they split. For the first time in a long time, she was defenseless. Cancer had knocked that strong, take-charge woman on her ass, so handling the uncertainties that lay ahead needed to be put aside for a moment.

I decided to reach out to Theresa, hoping to reignite our once-close bond. She told me our sister, Phyllis, was going to take her to get her nails done. If I could say one thing about Theresa, she never left the house without her hair done, makeup, and nails perfect. She had a ruby-red pantsuit and heels to match that she fondly called her "power suit," which she wore to business meetings and interviews.

"I'm tired and in lots of pain," she claimed. "Phyllis thinks a little pampering will be a good distraction."

I arrived at the nail salon first and waited in my car. When Phyllis pulled up, a frail, neon-yellow, skinny version of my sister was visible in the passenger's seat. She was weak and needed assistance just to get out of the car. Trying not to seem shocked by her appearance, I got out of my car, walked over to her, and gave her a hug. We talked as if no time had passed, and I tried to lighten the mood with a joke about her new, uncanny Winnie the Pooh appearance as we entered the salon. She giggled, holding her side in agony. I sat on a low stool next to her while she got her nails done. She could barely make it through the appointment, putting her head down on the table for some relief.

From across the nail salon, I looked at Phyllis to see she was visibly upset. She shook her head at me, almost in disbelief. I looked up at the clock on the wall over Theresa's head as it ticked loudly, second by second. I tried to shove the thoughts from my mind that her grave condition might steal our sister from us.

Later that day, I telephoned Mom. She was still unwilling to believe her daughter was so sick. Her dismissive way of handling bad news still struck me as odd. Dad, while we were growing up, worked long hours and always seemed inevitably focused on supporting his family. On the other hand, Mom was an amazingly strong woman, but she was also an emotional cripple. We always knew she loved us, but emotionally revealing herself was something that never occurred, especially when we were younger.

Unable to eat due to the obstruction, Theresa drank liquids and lived on blended foods. I worried she would not be able to sustain herself and succumb to her condition because of weakness and dehydration. In the mountain of my emotions, I decided I needed to go see her to offer my help. Whether it was for culinary assistance or just someone to talk to, I wanted to help her any way I could.

When I arrived, she greeted me at the door, barely able to hold herself up. I stepped inside. Theresa stood about five-foot-two. Her once curvy frame was now a tiny woman encased in a long, blue, triple-X large man's T-shirt that almost touched the floor. I helped her to the couch, and she laid her head back in pain.

In her late thirties, she started wearing hairpieces. She had thin hair as a child, and I think the desire to have long, luscious locks drove her to wear wigs. That day, the wig was off. Her natural hair was a mousy brown and pulled back tight in a thin ponytail. Trying not to throw up, she sat motionless on the grease-stained couch.

When I was finally able to look at the surroundings, I was shocked at where she was staying. The house was in such disarray and reminded me of an air freshener commercial; smells okay but what a mess! As we talked, all I could think was that my sister was fighting for her life in that depressing environment. A bit of a clean freak, I have been known to overreact, but this wasn't well lived in or controlled chaos. It was a certifiable pigpen. I feared the precarious living conditions would put her health at more risk, and she was alone most of the time.

I have always tried to be someone you could count on in a crisis. My desire to help has always been more than superficial. My heart was broken for her. My sister, the one whom I once shared so many fun times growing up, needed me. I owed it to her, along with myself, to be front and center in her impending journey through what was to come.

"Maybe you should consider coming to live with Matt and me," I offered, thinking I could take much better care of her if she were living with me. "Besides, you probably don't want to burden Veronica with taking care of you," I said. "She's young and already has enough to worry about. I know deep in your heart you don't want to put her through this."

Theresa nodded in agreement, refraining from verbally responding.

"Think about it." I smiled. "It'll be like old times."

However, my opinions ran deeper. I was concerned for her well-being. Yet, I held those thoughts back when I made the offer. I could see it in her eyes; she knew I would be her best chance at survival. I suspected that she felt the stress of staying with them as well, but was hesitant about expressing her feelings.

She took in a deep breath and sighed. "Everything is always so complicated; I think dying is going to be a whole lot easier than living."

Taken aback by her response, she already seemed keenly aware that she was very sick. I could see she was in a tremendous amount of discomfort. She leaned over and held her side.

"I've got you covered," I told her. That would be my mantra from that day forward.

Chapter 4

Reeling with pain and intense vomiting compelled her to meet with Doctor Reeves, a surgeon highly regarded in the field of hepatobiliary. Being in the medical field herself, she knew all too well that her condition was serious.

He would figure out what was going on with her, and she could continue attaining more and more success. She forecasted her relationship with him to be short. She knew from her research he was highly competent and would surely get to the bottom of the rapid weight loss, intense aching, and relentless retching that plagued her for over a month.

She convinced herself she didn't need to get to know him or like him. His reputation spoke for itself. He was considered extremely intelligent and a crusader in his field. When the door opened to the exam room, a handsome, tall, well-dressed man, wearing a white lab coat appeared. The slight hint of dark circles under his eyes provided a glimpse into the long hours he spent working. His face showed his passionate, fierce work ethic, which we would soon find out as the relationship grew.

Once past the introductions, he was markedly concerned with Theresa's condition. We all sat quietly as the doctor stared at the CT scan images displayed on the computer screen. When I think back to this day, I cannot help but think she knew she was dying. Theresa sat steady; knowing full well he wasn't going to tell her all she needed was a taste of normal life and relaxation to put her fatigued body back on track. We watched as he glanced through the slides. For what seemed like an eternity, he rolled back in his chair and faced her directly, with his knees almost touching hers.

"Theresa."

"It's okay, just tell me." She seemed to console him.

"You have pancreatic cancer."

The weight of what he revealed was heavy. Her eyes closed and opened slowly. I could see the last bit of vivacity collapse. She extended her hand and touched his as if *she* had given *him* the bad news.

My heart pounded in my chest. I wanted to hate him for giving my sister such horrible news. I looked over at Margaret, as she tried to hold back the well of water filling her eyes.

Theresa was fully aware of the death sentence she had just been handed. However, her reaction was very calm; I think her body went numb. The question of "How are you feeling?" would now take on a much-graver implication. Her face never showed any real sadness. Living with a death sentence would now become perhaps the biggest goal she had set for herself. In Theresa fashion, she would push back the bleak cloud hanging over her head and focus on maintaining normality for those around her, now feeling the urgency to get her affairs together for her children.

Her grave condition was not changing her life, but rather crushing it in an instant. It was as if the path she laid out for herself had been demolished, leaving her with the daunting task of how she would work around it for the sake of the two most important people in her life: her kids.

Life had finally shifted toward success, but in that instant, she would have to face the fact that all her planning for the future would fall by the wayside. She feared her chance to give her children a fabulous life would go unfinished.

I could see the wheels turning as she tried to accept the harsh reality that her time was limited. Doctor Reeves told her about a surgical procedure called the Whipple. He explained that this procedure could provide a means to prevent cancer from spreading, along with prolonging her life. Those who undergo this Whipple procedure successfully at the five-year mark have a twenty-five percent survival rate. Theresa was strong-willed and resolute not to let this cancer get the best of her.

"I'll take the five-year plan," she proclaimed. "I'll do what I know how to do best; stand up and fight." She held it together, clenching her teeth and giving him a half smile.

Knowing her critical condition, he grinned, happy to see she was up for the challenge that lay ahead. He could tell she was smart, curious, and determined. I had never been more proud or honored to be with someone than I was with her that day. She was so multifaceted; she chose life and to adapt to her condition. Rather than hiding her head in the sand, she chose to face her fate head-on.

There wasn't any hesitation from her whether to do the surgery. It wasn't *when* for her. As she has done so many times in the past, the world kicked her in the ass and she came back swinging. She asked him several questions, not about the procedure, but what her chances were in his eyes, and if any of his patients have died during the operation.

Theresa was in tremendous discomfort so she would lie down, but sat up frequently. Doctor Reeves spoke in a calm but confident voice and explained all the questions she threw at him. He stressed that her strength for the surgery was key, and over the next few weeks, she needed to get her endurance up for the lengthy ten-hour procedure; two thousand calories were the goal. We were on a mission. He gave her hope that her future might still hold a positive outcome. Realizing how thin she had gotten in the last few months, she needed to bulk up.

"I'm going to get myself in tip-top shape," Theresa said. "I've got this."

Doctor Reeves excused himself from the room for a moment. Without a word spoken, Theresa got up from the exam table and ventured over to the stainless steel sink in the corner of the room. Hunched over the basin, she held her forehead as she viciously dry-heaved. Margaret and I sat quietly while she splashed cool water on her face.

Shortly after, the nurse came in with all her pre-op. February 16 was the date of the surgery. Labs needed to be done, as well as another CT scan to make sure the cancer was not visible in any other organs prior to the day of surgery. Doctor Reeves returned, giving Theresa the opportunity to ask any additional questions. She did not dodge any details about her condition.

"What is the prognosis if you cannot perform the surgery?" she asked.

He steadily responded, "Three to six months."

Despite the tragic diagnosis, it was strangely liberating for her to know what had been plaguing her body for the last few months, and she knew she was in good hands. Although there was a strong possibility that the cancer had spread to other organs and he would be unable to perform the surgery, she kept her mind positive and pure.

The moment we left his office, there was no question in my mind that I would be front and center to help her battle this beast. I put my arm around her as we walked out of his office. She rested her head on my shoulder, and without any words spoken, she knew I would be her biggest ally. That day changed both our lives in a way neither of us would have ever imagined. When I look back on our time as kids, it seemed as if our close bond had a deeper meaning. Our entire time growing up was preparing us for this challenge.

One day she was fighting for a better life for herself and her family, and the next, she was simply just fighting to live. In the blink of an eye, the past had vanished, leaving her with wondering how she would conquer the future that lay ahead in the face of her own mortality.

When we drove off toward the sunset in Margaret's car, the silence was profound. I didn't say much, not because I wasn't sure what to say, but rather, I knew Theresa was processing and planning.

Margaret broke the silence. "You have done so many amazing things in your life. We will get through this." She meant well, but Theresa's mind was elsewhere.

Theresa didn't utter a response, but rather nodded in agreement. Resting her head against the window, taking in the last bit of sun gleaming through the windshield, she knew she would never fulfill her dream of being a CEO of a major hospital. She had just begun to feel the reality of all her hopes and dreams, and now they would remain just that—dreams. Now, how she chose to live her life from this day forward would define the difference between success and failure.

Knowing her sister's life would be cut short was now unmistakable, and Margaret could feel the sorrow choking off her air. It was like being trapped in a maze, unable to decide which direction was the correct one to follow. Encourage her sister that everything would be okay, or face the harsh reality that we would only have a limited time with her and try to make the best of the worst situation?

This devastating news would transform our entire family, so Margaret did what she had done so many times when we were growing up; she chose to comfort and protect her sister. Whatever that would mean as time moved forward, she would face the task and be there for her.

With that simple nod from Theresa, Margaret knew what she had to do—be the best big sister she could be. Nothing changed from when we were kids. She was just a little older, and, hopefully, a little stronger and wiser.

Growing up, Margaret was the protector, always ready to defend the honor of her family. The girls in the neighborhood loved her, and the boys feared her. She wouldn't hesitate about chasing one of them down in the street if they wronged her little sisters. She was the one who cried for us when we were sad or being tormented, but would turn into a raging bull if anyone messed with her siblings. She was freakishly strong for a young girl, and if she came after you, you had better take off running. With her teeth firmly pressed around her tongue, she could deliver a punch that would bring stars to your eyes.

I remember one instance when us girls were in the garage having a fashion show. Margaret and Sophie had set up the garage like a stage. They hung sheets over the opening of the garage, and we paraded around, coming in and out from behind the drapes. As Theresa rounded the corner in her plastic Barbie heels and mini dress, one of the boys in the neighborhood thought it would be funny to lift the sheet and throw a rolled-up newspaper at her—something he would live to regret. Barely off the driveway, Margaret and Sophie tore out of the garage, tackling him on the parkway near the gutter. Margaret held him down as Sophie dunked the newspaper in the disgusting murky gutter water, slapping it back and forth across his cheeks. Painted with scum across his face and down his shirt, he ran back to the boys that put him up to the task. They quickly dispersed as Margaret shook her hand and yelled out a stern warning. Today was no different. She was there for her little sister in a time of crisis and would do anything to help her through what was coming.

It was well after 6:00 p.m. Theresa was scheduled for a temporary feeding tube in the morning. Hoping to get in as many calories daily, Doctor Reeves suggested this might be a good option since she struggled to keep down simple liquids.

Having this feeding tube placed proved to be overwhelming. Theresa's coping mechanism always seemed to be intact ... except for that morning. Although temporary, I don't think she was truly ready for the outcome. When she emerged, the shock on her face was almost too much to handle. She was barely able to hold herself up. I could not ignore the look of defiance on her face, along with the tears trapped inside her eyes. It seemed as if she would crumble under the despair of having this rubber hose loosely taped across her cheek, up her nose, and down her throat.

The radiologist gave her a hug and handed her off to me. "This will help you until the surgery," he remarked.

She nodded, unable to speak for fear of breaking into hysterical sobbing. Oftentimes, the unspoken word has a much greater impact than that of the words themselves. Theresa was clearly defeated, and the word "until" revealed his state of mind about her condition.

Then, what? I wondered. Until what?

Until she's dead? Until she's able to eat? Until another setback? Until she's cured? Such a tiny word harboring a vast meaning of unknowns.

The questions continued to roll around in my head. I kept the thoughts quiet as we left the hospital. Once outside in the afternoon air, she seemed to sober up to the reality of this hose limply adorning on her face.

It was at that moment I think the whole severity of the situation came crashing down on her. This cancer was now encapsulating her life. Her self-preservation had always served her well, acknowledging her limitations and strong points in a bad situation. Caught between frustration and worry, she began to weep.

"I can't do this," she insisted. "I just don't think I can do this."

We scheduled an appointment to see Doctor Reeves that afternoon before going back home. Theresa went deep inside herself and said nothing on the car ride to Margaret's house. When we got back to the house, she lay on the couch. If she tried to utter anything, she seemed to choke on the tube that ran down her throat.

"I cannot keep this thing in," she said abruptly. "It has to come out."

Her decision was final. She wanted the tube gone. I told her to call the doctor and maybe they could get this worked out before our afternoon appointment. Doctor Reeves got on the phone after a short time and assured her the gagging sensation would subside, but if she couldn't tolerate it, to take out the tube.

"So either you'll have it, or you won't when I see you in a few hours," he claimed.

That proved to be the green light for Theresa. Without hesitation, she got up from the couch and stormed to the bathroom. Removing that tube herself seemed barbaric; however, desperate times called for desperate measures. With what only seemed like a split second, she emerged from the bathroom. Noticeably absent was the tube. She calmly lay back down on the couch.

"There," she said. "Much better."

Sitting in his office, we made small talk until the doctor emerged. Theresa was worried he'd be upset that she'd yanked out the feeding tube.

"I guess you couldn't take it." He grinned. "No worries. You are looking much better than yesterday. Try to get in as many calories as you can with the protein drinks."

He explained to her he that he would place a feeding tube directly into her stomach when he does the surgery, which will be much easier to manage than having a tube flopping from her face. On this appointment, there was a medical student shadowing him in the exam room, a young, slender man no more than twenty-five years old. Doctor Reeves quizzed him with a barrage of questions regarding her condition. As he stammered for the right answer, Theresa mouthed the response, trying to help the struggling student.

With a heavy heart, she slowly accepted her fate, knowing any time she wasted on how to prolong her life only took away from the time she had left. She drew strength from the characters in the novels she loved so much; her destiny would depend on her response.

That afternoon when we got back home, I decided to pay my parents a visit. I needed to explain to them the intensity of Theresa's condition. Mom sat quietly awaiting Dad's reaction to the news. A staunch, retired businessman, his first reaction was to inquire if her financial affairs were in order.

"Does she have a will or living trust?"

I told him I would find out, and if not, I would help her find someone to handle her business matters. I told him to speak to her himself, that if he wanted to help her, he should call her, but he ignored my suggestion, putting the tasks on me as if I said nothing.

"If she doesn't have these things in place, we will pay for the attorney," he stated.

I guess everyone saw a different scenario of what was happening to our family. My siblings were facing losing a sister, my parents were struggling to make amends with their once-estranged daughter, and I seemed to be caught somewhere in the middle, trying to help my sister live her life while fighting the day-to-day drama of those closest to her.

I was sure she would fight and wouldn't die soon, but it would be faster than anyone would be able to accept. I know she had so many things she would love to do, but the harsh thing about cancer is, not only are your days numbered, your energy is sucked out of you like siphoning gas from a car. One minute you are moving along, and the next, you are running on empty. I know having your affairs in order when you are about to die should be top of the list, but it just seems so petty in the grand scheme of things.

The silence in the room was deafening. The reality of losing my sister intensified. Tensions were high for me, and before I said something I might regret, I chose to leave their house and let them sort through their emotions.

It seems, as we get older, things get so much more complicated with family. "Family is for kids," I always say. I guess maybe because you don't have the inclination to question the demands made on you.

Chapter 5

Over the next few weeks, Theresa was spending more time at my house. Although she was still showing signs of jaundice, she seemed to gain some of her strength back. Her face was no longer drawn and sallow; the yellow hue was fading. I only realized she still glowed when I saw someone staring at her. She told me she would take me up on my offer to stay with us. I was glad she made that choice. This period before the surgery would give her time to relax and get ready for the challenge that lay ahead.

We went to Veronica's to pick up a few things. Since Theresa had been helping them financially, she worried they might take her leaving the wrong way. But, she told Veronica she would still give her money each week. Focused on taking care of herself, she knew she was facing a huge task ahead of her. It was clear Veronica was upset, as she suspected the living conditions were driving her to me. They cleaned up and made a more living-friendly environment. Yet, that didn't alter Theresa's decision, assuring them it was less chaotic and a little calmer for her at my house.

The air was fresh outside. It was cloudy, not enough to cause rain, but a slight drizzle. I felt the drops hitting my cheeks as I loaded Theresa's possessions into the back seat. I ran back inside to grab the last few items, while Theresa waited in the car. The mist made the grass quite wet, causing me to slip and slide as I made my way back and forth. Theresa smiled through the passenger window, probably hoping to get a front-row seat to my taking a tumble. Without incident, however, we headed back to the house.

Theresa seemed to crave the change of peacefulness and security that my home offered. There is a saying that your senses are much more in sync when someone is relying on you for safety. Now that she was with me, I felt a presence. Perhaps it was a guardian angel watching over me, helping me with navigating these unchartered waters.

Mom had two turtledoves that had made her backyard their home for several years. I was not sure if they were the same two birds, but she insisted they were her parents, who had passed several years ago. Strangely enough, since Theresa had been staying with me, I, too, had a set of turtledoves that seemed to have made my yard their home.

I purchased a bird feeder to convince my new friends to stay with us. Our backyard soon became a haven for many birds. All sorts of birds filled the magnificent Jacaranda tree planted in my yard, including one small, orange-breasted canary I was sure was a rogue pet from someone in the neighborhood. Diving down from the branches, they fed, and then rushed back up onto the vast limbs. The lilac blanket left behind from the blooms falling from the tree was a heavenly sight, and the birds loved their cozy dwelling.

While all the birds came and went, the doves remained close to home. One morning, I noticed a bundle of twigs nestled in a tree in the backyard. Realizing she had built a nest, I observed her from my bedroom window in the evening hours sitting on her eggs, while her mate kept a close watch nearby. I was happy they, too, felt comfortable to make my home their permanent residence.

Over the next few days, Theresa's sleeping increased. Perhaps she was conserving energy for the upcoming marathon. I set a clock to wake her to drink a protein shake, and then within a few minutes, she would fall back off to sleep. While I thought she might have given up, she seemed to look better and better each day. Her formula seemed to be working.

Our dog, Riley, became Theresa's guard dog, remaining close by her side. I sensed he took his job very seriously, keeping an eye out for anyone trying to take her from us. When her bedroom door was ajar, I listened to her talking to him in a quiet voice, and I could hear his dog tags jingle when she rubbed the back of his neck.

"Keep me safe, Riley," she said. "Don't leave me."

Saturday morning, she woke up on her own. I heard her rustling around in the bedroom. I knocked on the door and entered in one motion. She wasn't in her bed. In a panic, my eyes darted around the room. In the bathroom stood my sister; dressed as if she were going out for the day. Riley lay at the edge of the carpet watching her while she swiped on the last stroke of mascara.

"You okay?" I inquired.

"Yep. Can you drive me to the store? I need to get some hand weights. I tried to use water bottles to do my arm curls, but they are too slippery."

I thought she was screwing with me. All this time she was in here training for this event, while I thought she was sleeping. I shook my head. She amazed me each day with her resilience and passion.

When she was young, she always seemed uneasy about herself; what we viewed as lack of confidence was her way of knowing she needed to push herself to strive for more. She wanted success, she wanted to love and a sense of making a difference in the lives around her.

It was another day of daunting tests before the surgery. We spent the night before at Margaret's house so we wouldn't have to make the two-hour, painstaking drive in the morning. Also, Theresa wanted to see Margaret's husband, Hank; together for over forty years, we joked, *He's our brother from another mother.*

We arrived at the hospital once again, this time for a CT scan with contrast. We checked in, and the nurse came out with what looked like a gallon of dye. Theresa's eyes widened as she glanced around for a trash can, knowing she would struggle not to throw it all up. If I could just step back from the situation, watching her try to keep anything down was hard to believe. It was like there was a cork inside her, not allowing things to pass. Once she would put something in her mouth, the power-struggle with her body to keep it down would ensue.

The day of surgery was fast approaching. Even with all the loose ends she was trying to tie up before that day, she found the need to make provisions for Derek, concerned he wouldn't make it to the surgery on time. He seemed like such a simple person, plodding along throughout the day with no real direction. He moved as slow as anyone could without rolling backward. His six-foot-five frame lumbered along most days, and I wondered if he was even alert most of the time. But, for some reason, she once had something for him, and this was neither the time nor the place to judge or ask questions.

Baggy, knee-length shorts and an array of neon-colored T-shirts made up his wardrobe. All he needed was a vest, and he would be mistaken for a crossing guard. He kept the shoestrings in his tennis shoes barely tied so he could slip in and out of them at a moment's notice, much like a firefighter waiting for an emergency call. I wondered why he had now become so determined to be by Theresa's side. Before she got sick, I think it was the mere fact she let him go without looking back. But, my suspicious mind felt there was, perhaps, a monetary element he might have been pursuing.

As I waited for Theresa to finish in the radiology lab, I admired the amazing beauty of the hospital. The building felt like it had a life all its own, protecting those who dwelled inside it. With its sprawling layout and multiple levels, the view out of the vast windows highlighted the well-kept landscape designed to make those who entered feel serene and welcome. Yet, staring out the gaping windows, I couldn't help but feel judged by the surrounding neighborhood outside the compound, which was more than a bit sketchy.

Theresa opted to get a room for Derek, herself, Veronica, and Clark at the hotel across the street from the medical center. Derek's persistence let him back in her life and—out of guilt or fatigue—she caved into the idea of having him around.

It killed me not to say something, but I kept my opinion about him quiet. He was neither my concern nor a formidable opponent I couldn't handle. Theresa was with me, and I would protect her from the long arm of his motives. Perhaps she needed the emotional support from a man. Whatever it was, I didn't understand it. What little I knew, he seemed like an opportunist. But, it was her life, so I stayed silent, all while keeping a close eye on him.

We rang the doorbell at the outside of the hotel lobby and a woman buzzed us in. It was a quaint, bed-and-breakfast-style hotel, but you got the feeling the daytime hours were okay, but the nightlife was a bit different. A burning candle on the lobby counter tried to mask the rampant, "dirty laundry" smell that ricocheted around the room, finding refuge up my nose.

As I stood in the lobby and Theresa was prepaying for the rooms, I could feel someone standing between us. I glanced over my shoulder, thinking it might be someone else that entered the foyer, but no one was there. This was the beginning of frequent visits by a procession of spirits. From childhood through adulthood, I frequently felt a presence that I was not alone. Perhaps a guardian angel or something giving me security when times were tough. It had been a while since I had "visitors," but it was clear they were back. In the well-lit lobby, a tall, gray figure stood between us, disappearing as quickly as it came.

A few days before surgery, Theresa received a call from Doctor Reeves, giving her the go-ahead. "There doesn't seem to be any issues with your CT scan. We are good for surgery."

Theresa was suffering on the long drive home. By the time we reached the house, after plodding through the freeway traffic, she was struggling with the unrelenting pain that had been a continuing affliction. Over the last few weeks, she endured back spasms with fluctuating intensity. It went from trivial pain to pain so agonizing that I would find her bent over her bed in tears, begging for some relief.

I told her she should rest when we got home, but with the good news that the Whipple was on, she wanted to go shopping and look for a bathing suit.

"I need to get something great to wear," she insisted. "When I am feeling better after surgery, we're taking a trip to Hawaii."

With that said, we made a beeline for the nearest shopping mall. I went to the Information Desk and checked out a wheelchair. The woman looked at me, then at my sister, wondering who needed the ride. By all outward appearance, Theresa looked good, causing us to get the stink-eye.

"I'll need a picture identification from both of you," the woman scolded. "And, a credit card."

She acted as if we would steal it or something. We didn't mind the drilling. It made Theresa happy, knowing she still looked good enough to hide she was dying.

It was the afternoon before her surgery. Theresa and I stopped by my parents' house. My mom wasn't doing well. Since she was struggling with her health, she decided she couldn't make it to the hospital. Theresa gave her a big hug and told her not to worry. Breaking their embrace, she stared at Mom.

"You don't look so good. Everything okay?" It was at that moment the distance between them seemed to fade. Dad appeared from the back of the house. With no words spoken, he hugged them both tight.

"We'll be right here waiting for you," he said.

I knew it was time for us to go. Theresa was holding herself together for them, but she needed to worry about herself now. I escorted her from the house and helped her into the front seat of the car. As we drove off, I could see tears rolling down her cheeks. Even during the most difficult time of her life, she worried about them.

We met up with Sophie to venture down to Margaret's house. Sophie offered to drive and the three of us laughed and talked the whole two hours. She gave us the usual white-knuckle ride; it was always an adventure of excitement and fright wrapped up in one escapade.

As a free spirit, Sophie never worries about how her actions might affect someone. Not in a selfish way, though. She does her own thing without thinking about what anyone thinks, which is an attribute many admire about her, or perhaps an attribute some might find offensive. While we all consider ourselves fashionable, Sophie has great taste in fashion, but loves to run around in flip-flops and cut-offs when there isn't anything going on. She's quite busty and lets her hair run wild in a curly, beach-wave style. Some days, she would look like she stepped off the sand, while other days she would look like a forgotten doll stuffed in a toy box.

After catching her husband of thirty-something years of cheating, Sophie endured a bitter divorce, so her dating skills were rusty. I laughed hard as Theresa gave her some sisterly dating advice.

"Avoid the banana peel," she joked, holding her side through the laughter.

"What is that?" she demanded. "Tell me."

Theresa fought to speak through the cackling and told us about one of her dating trysts with an uncircumcised lover.

"It was like having sex with someone that had a magic show. It was as if it was coming out of hibernation.

"The whole flap thing is really weird. The worst part of it

all was he wanted to convince me it made him a better lover. It didn't, and on top of it all, he was wearing tighty-whities.

"Just stay away, I'm warning you." She proclaimed, "You can't handle the responsibility."

Sophie looked in her rearview mirror at me cracking up. "Have you seen one?" she inquired, as if it were a UFO sighting.

"Nope, haven't had the honor," I vowed.

It was hard to believe my sister was about to go through a tremendous surgery she might not even live through, despite the fact the surgery was just a Band-Aid on her inevitable fate. But, for now, we were going to laugh long and hard, sharing stories and just being sisters.

Margaret had arranged a barbeque for family and friends that might want to come to hang out. Everyone stood amazed as Theresa entered the house, looking almost normal. Her eyes were a clear blue; cheeks were rosy, and only a glimmer of pain seemed apparent. My brother, James, didn't make the trek; he had bronchitis. Phyllis arrived shortly after us. I could see she was trying to fight her sad feelings.

"I can't stop crying," she said. "I cried the whole way here." She wiped her eyes from under her sunglasses. "I had to drive around the block a few times just to get myself together."

Her sadness vanished when she saw how great Theresa looked. I gave her a hug, and she settled into the fun with the rest of us. Phyllis is not an emotional person. Most of the time, she maintains her composure. So, when that rare window opened and she showed you how she felt, it caught you off guard. I think Theresa getting sick changed all of us, and she was not excluded from that.

The time we had flew by. Theresa and her clan left around

7:30 p.m. to head over to the hotel. She was not looking forward to drinking the GoLYTLEY to flush her system before tomorrow's surgery. Drinking a gallon of salted water in her condition would not fare well. Not long after they left, she called me in panic.

"I can't choke this stuff down. Every time I swallow even the smallest amount, it jets right back up."

With conviction, I responded, "I'm sure they have provisions for situations like this, trust me. They always do. Besides, you have only been drinking liquids. How much poop could be in there?"

"You'd think, right?"

"Get some rest; everything will be fine."

Reassured by my confidence, she released a nervous chuckle and hung up the phone.

That night, Phyllis opted to stay at a hotel ... not sure what that was all about.

"I need time to get ready and do my hair," she claimed.

"It takes you an hour to do that mess?" Sophie retorted.

Phyllis ignored her and left for the hotel. Sophie is the person you need to keep a close watch on. Like a three-year-old, you never know what's coming out of her mouth, and it's not always tactful.

Sophie and I shared the vast king bed in the master bedroom. I hunkered in under the down blankets, while she flailed her legs under and over of the covers, snoring like a bear in hibernation, while Margaret slept on the trundle in the spare room.

Chapter 6

When we arrived at the hospital around 4:30 a.m., everyone met up on the second floor, which was vacant of people, to settle in for the long day ahead. Theresa and the gang showed up a few minutes later, and we stretched out on the U-shaped sofa.

Around 6:30 a.m., a nurse called her name to take her for surgery. The nurse came over, put on her plastic wristband, and verified the information. "Okay, follow me."

Exhaustion blanketed Theresa's face. She longed to lie down to gather her strength. At that moment, the future she would soon face was upon her, and the future dreams she had once imagined for herself would vanish behind those hospital doors.

Her life was now compressed into one fleeting moment, as she said goodbye to each of us. She gave me a hug and held me tightly. "Thank you for everything." Those were the words that defined her and everything she stood for; appreciating what life she had now, not dwelling over the life she would now leave behind. Her future was receding; faced with only one thing at that moment: *Would she survive to see another day?*

Let me just say my days leading up to the surgery I was feeling very doubtful of her condition. My gut was telling me she was not going to make it through it, or they wouldn't be able to perform the surgery, or complications...something... I just knew the day wasn't going to go as planned. When she said, "Thank you for everything," it felt like her last goodbye.

The doctors would do the exploratory procedure first, to make sure her cancer had not metastasized to adjacent areas, which would take about an hour. There was nothing to do now but wait. I reflected on these last few weeks, how my sister, against all odds, pushed herself away from death. If we truly have the power to choose life, she did, and now the next few hours would define how her life was going to move forward.

Clark had been programming the channel on the television with his cell phone, which was mildly annoying and entertaining at the same time. Never, in her wildest dreams, did Theresa think her daughter would end up with the likes of Clark. He was a tall, slender man, with ears that didn't seem to go with his waiflike figure, spanning halfway up the side of his head, seeming to start at his neck. With his belt cinched tight and his watch running halfway up his arm because it was too big, he was no stranger to alcohol abuse, his constant fidgeting and obnoxious interruptions could make even the calmest person crazy.

So, when Derek decided to take Veronica and Clark to Denny's for breakfast, it was a bit of a relief. Christopher was away at college and still unaware of his mother's grave condition. Theresa insisted on keeping him in the dark until after the long, grueling surgery. We were all preparing for the ten-plus hours ahead so a quick bite seemed like no big deal.

Sophie scavenged at the vending machine and returned with chips and a drink. Airports and hospitals always seem to bring out the most horrible habits in the early-morning hours. She pulled one of the chips from the bag. It had three clear black marks on it, making the shape of a smiley face. She held it up to her cheek, grinning.

"Theresa is smiling at us."

By this point, patients and visitors filled the surgical area; the once-quiet area was now very busy. Knowing the surgery required the insertion of a camera in the abdomen to check for metastasis, I paced the hallway for the first hour or so, hoping they found nothing in the surrounding areas that would subsequently cancel the procedure. As I glanced at the large clock on the wall, my thoughts were that plenty of time had passed since she was taken in, and surely, the surgery must be now underway for at least an hour. We all stretched out in the area we had claimed as our own, awaiting the news.

I will never forget the next moment because it felt like time stood still. Coming down the hallway from surgery was Theresa's doctor and another physician. He was carrying a wood box that looked like something you would make in a high school wood shop. When I saw the doctor, I looked over at Sophie. We both seemed to have the same thoughts without saying them out loud. Should we run or tell him to go away? His presence could only be a bad thing ... She died during surgery, or the surgery was unsuccessful. He motioned to all of us to follow him into a private room adjacent to the waiting area.

"Come with me," he insisted.

Single file, we all went into the small, enclosed room and sat nervously waiting for him to speak.

"I have some bad news. The cancer has spread, and I was unable to perform the surgery."

He explained the events in detail, but I'm sure I stopped listening once he said there was nothing he could do. My attention focused on the worn brown box he clasped in front of him. I hoped he might have some magic fairy dust in there he was going to sprinkle over her and make it all better. But, it was just his surgical loupes; not a hidden magic potion.

I tried to listen, but anything he had to say at that point meant nothing. The bottom line was ... She was dying. It was only a matter of time. I asked a few minor questions, and then someone, I am not sure whom, said, "So what can we expect?" He stated if she made it to Christmas it would be a gift. That was only ten short months from now. Phyllis completely broke down, Sophie quietly cried, and I could feel a stream of tears roll down my face as Margaret thanked him for being so gentle and kind to our sister. There was nothing more to say.

"I'll give you a minute."

He left the room, and we all stood there in shock for a moment, and then hugged one another. Derek stood with his back against the wall in disbelief. Clark, however, seemed like he was in the wrong room. No emotion whatsoever. Maneuvering something on his phone, he barely looked up. He didn't even hug Veronica, which I couldn't help but find extremely odd.

Doctor Reeves emerged once again. "I told her I was unable to do the surgery," he said. "She is pretty out of it, though, so I am not sure how much she grasped. If you want, you can say nothing to her and let me handle it. Whichever you prefer. I will be back to check on her later. She will be in recovery for a while."

Clearly, you could feel his disappointment. We think doctors can disconnect themselves from their patients, but I knew in her short time with him he had developed a special connection to her. Although he fought the feelings, it affected him, too.

We all took turns going into recovery to see her. She was calm, considering the outcome of the procedure, almost as if she knew this day would end in either death or failure. Hooked up to several tubes and, clearly, on pain medication, she seemed surprisingly alert. Her concerns lay more with us and with how Mom and Dad took the news. I spoke briefly outside the room with my husband. He had contacted a cancer treatment center, anxious to help and find out what her options might be. He gave me the telephone number to call to speak with the administrator to educate myself and possibly ease some of the tasks that might lie ahead. Cancer would continue to separate Theresa from the life she had fought so hard to obtain. Helping her through that process would now be the most important task.

While I cannot speak to all cancer centers, I can say, with strong certainty, that this cancer center was solely a comfort to death when it came to cancer as voracious as pancreatic cancer. The woman, Emma, tried hard to convince me this was the best option for my sister at this point.

"We can keep her comfortable while she goes through the process of healing."

I pressed her hard about what she was telling me. "So, is there anything you do that would prolong her life?" She avoided my direct questions, so I pressed her harder. "Is there *anything* you would do other than comfort care?"

After several rounds of the same conversation, she finally admitted, "No. Just comfort and nutritional care."

I thanked her for her time. Yet, I was so angry—not that she couldn't help my sister, but rather, she was trying to convince me they were somehow her savior, her life preserver.

I was very disappointed, not just for our situation, but for the many people that watch those commercials and think somehow these places are a miracle cure, when, in fact, they are just a means to live out your last days on earth.

Somehow, Emma still felt some need, perhaps, to defend her position. "It's very difficult taking care of a terminal patient," she insisted. "We don't judge families that need to leave their loved ones to the professionals."

A rage stirred inside of me. Was she implying I should now abandon my sister at their doorstep because it would just be easier? I openly expressed to her that while sometimes people can't take care of a loved one, if you can, you should.

"I can take care of my sister and give her the best care for however many days she might have ahead of her," I vowed. "I am certainly not going to have her live with strangers in her final days, out of convenience."

"This is a great thing you are going to try to tackle for your sister." She stated, "I hope you are up for the challenge until the end."

There was that word again ... "*until*." Like there is just simply a wave of silence and emptiness until the end. I may not be able to save her, but we were going to give her a hell of a good time until she was ready to leave us.

Without hesitation, I sharply responded, "It isn't a great thing; it's the *right* thing."

I paced the halls after my conversation with her, thinking that perhaps my emotions were making me a bit callous to her perseverance to provide alternatives. I chose to phone her back to apologize. As heartbroken as I was, it didn't seem right to take it out on her. She was just doing her job; a service many people choose to utilize.

However, my sister was never going to a cancer center.

She would remain with me until she took her last breath. I knew I didn't need to search for a solution to her care. I had that covered. For now, I would keep my feelings tucked safely in my heart. I promised myself I would not show Theresa my sadness but rather show her my strength to help her fight.

Although the surgery was unsuccessful, an incision from chest to pelvis remained due to the exploratory aspect of the procedure, which would keep her in the hospital for about a week.

The nurses were changing shifts. Theresa was tired. She laid her head back in pain.

"You okay?" I asked.

"Yep, just trying to get comfortable."

I could see, for the first time that day, the significance of what she would soon be facing was sinking in. One day she was a successful businesswoman and the next, she was struggling to live.

"You guys should get going," she said. "You all look tired."

She motioned for Margaret to open the blinds so she could admire the light of the moon shining through her window. If there had just been a patch of grass for her to lie back on and stare up at the stars, it would have seemed like she was a kid again. It was a place where she let herself go to find peace. Today I think it was not just for peace but rather strength as well.

I must admit, I felt inadequate to her courage and the iron will she revealed. I couldn't help but think there would be a moment in time where, once again, the aspects of always having to struggle would wear down the totality of her collected experiences. I guess living in the thought of dying makes you more in tune with your mortality.

This would be an eye-opening experience for all of us.

How many times is one bestowed the job of facing their biggest fears head-on in their lifetime—and knowing there is no real positive solution? She would have the opportunity to reflect on all the happy times as well as the sad. Right any wrongs from her past and, more importantly, her biggest legacy would be leaving all of us with cherished memories.

The drive back to Margaret's house was quiet. We dropped Phyllis off at her hotel to gather her bag to come back to Margaret's house. Sophie and I remained in the backseat, letting Margaret chauffeur us back to the house. Aside from Sophie, I felt a presence next to me. I felt the strength of my invisible companion, but unsure of the message I was to take away from its existence.

As the late night manifested into the early morning, I lay in bed staring at the ceiling, worrying about my dying sister and thinking, *I know she feels she has so many unresolved issues in her life.* There was a sense now that words have true meaning, and that I, as her baby sister, needed to help her through whatever time she had left to resolve her most important tasks.

My job was to make her life as meaningful and fulfilling as possible in the face of what was to come. I understood now more than ever that she needed me. I would replace her weakness with my strength, fueling her determination while racing against time. The last thing I wanted was for her to die in pain, grappling to make some sense of her life with all the struggles and sacrifices she had endured.

The next morning, I stopped by the hospital and told her I needed to run back home to get things ready for her arrival. She was groggy. I stroked her arm, and she opened her eyes slowly, as a tear coursed down her cheek. I sensed the news of her failed surgery was now sinking in and the unexpected reality of dying was heavy on her mind.

"You'll be right back, though, right?" she whispered.

"Yep, as quick as I can."

Driving home alone, I tried to imagine what kind of pain she would have been in if she had the complex Whipple procedure. First, my thoughts were relief that she would endure no further suffering, then a troubling, heavy sense of clarity that I should have been hoping for the former. While my wish was for Doctor Reeves to save her, I knew this type of cancer had taken many people from their loved ones quickly and without warning. The obvious had now become unescapable. It was just a matter of when.

Chapter 7

I spent the day with my husband and our dog, Riley, my one-hundred-pound Boxer that had quickly forged a tremendous bond with Theresa. Matt and I had always lived in large homes but, recently, we had downsized and were now enjoying a smaller place. It became an inside joke between us that when we had all the room in the world no one visited. But, now in a smaller space, we have lots of company. My brother, James, had fallen on some hard times, and I offered to let him stay with us for a while to get on his feet. Now, a year later, he seemed hunkered down like a gopher with no signs of departing.

That evening would prove to be a turning point for me and limits of what I would and would not tolerate. Around two o'clock in the morning, Riley jumped up as if he saw something alarmed him. Standing rigid at the top of the stairs, he wouldn't budge. I caught a swift, overwhelming smell of smoke. I followed him and stood perfectly still, looking down from the top landing. The first thing that came to mind was someone broke into the house and had the nerve to be smoking.

Matt woke up and saw me standing there. "What's wrong?"

I walked back into the bedroom to tell him.

He said, "It isn't anyone. I had the same experience when you were away at the hospital."

I was instantly angry. My brother, a closet smoker, puffed away before he arrived home most nights, stinking of old cigarette ashes when he entered the house. Prior to now, I had tried to ignore it, figuring it was his business, but now, I would have my sister living here, and I didn't need her health compromised by anything.

"Do you think James is smoking?"

"I don't know."

I stormed downstairs, now sure it was James smelling up the house. Like a mouse in a maze, I ran from room to room, looking for signs of a burning cigarette. I decided to wake him, fully aware that he wasn't the best at noticing things. He would drop everything on the floor and wouldn't even realize it. All I could imagine was a lit cigarette rolling around on the carpet downstairs.

I called his name. "James. James." He woke out of a deep sleep. "Are you smoking?"

He came to the bedroom door, startled. "No, no, I'm not."

I explained to him the stench in the hallway. Knowing his history of sneaking around smoking, I could only think it was coming from him. He followed me around the house, trying to smell, but his sinuses were such a mess and his incessant coughing just proved to annoy me further. He apologized, but insisted he never smoked near the house.

I raised my hand like a stop sign. "Just go back to bed."

The smell did not let up. I went back to bed, Riley following close behind me. I tried to ignore the stink, but

I could still smell the rank odor. All I could think of was cleaning and spraying. I tried to fall asleep, but it was useless. I lay there for hours, with eyes wide open and a million thoughts running through my head. Finally, from exhaustion, I drifted off.

When I awoke, Matt was gone. He took Riley to the golf course to run with the other dogs. My spray fest ensued. I could still smell tiny elements of smoke. It permeated my nostrils. I no longer thought the house smelled; I was just obsessed.

James woke up and told me he was sorry. I think he figured it was easier to apologize than argue his point. I was still so disappointed and angry. I stood rigid in the kitchen while he tried to console me.

"You do realize your sister is probably dying from her years of smoking, right?"

Theresa had smoked in her twenties and thirties, which I feared was the catalyst to her cancer. I didn't let him answer as I continued with my tirade.

"And, here you are, still smoking at sixty years old. I am not doing this. You want to smoke? Let me just cover your face with a pillow and suffocate you now while you aren't suffering." I raged on. "Spare us all the pain of watching you die, because that is what *you're* headed for."

All too familiar was the outcome of someone suffering from the effects of smoking. Matt's dad died of emphysema, and it was a horrible death for him and those of us who watched him suffer a slow, arduous passing.

He tried to hug me tightly, but I squirmed out of his grasp. I needed some time to be alone, and his excuses weren't making it any easier. I walked away from him, leaving him standing alone in the kitchen. I needed to run away from my life for a while. I was mad, and I was frustrated and in need of some time away from my own thoughts. I took to the streets for a long, vigorous walk. I was walking so hard against the cement my heels were hurting. I had such an intense hatred for what was happening to my sister I wanted to cause harm to someone or something to release my anger. As time passed, I could finally feel my stride lighten and my heart stopped pounding. When I reached the house, no one was home. I jumped in the shower, welcoming the hot water beating on my neck, hoping the repetition of the drops would provide the longed-for calmness.

Later when Matt got home, we had a conversation about it. He told me that he was experiencing the same sort of thing. "He's either smoking, or my dad is back." We had lived in a house not long after Matt's dad passed where many strange and unexplained events led us to think he was present. I would have thought, no ... However, the two cutout figures I had seen recently led me to believe we had some "visitors." I don't mind, really; in fact, it feels comforting. I performed the white sage cleanse after the events of the day prior. I felt the need to rid the house of any negativity from unwanted guests, both dead and alive.

The next morning, I telephoned Theresa, and she said they were going to let her out of the hospital. Derek decided to drive her to the house so I didn't have to make the trip back. When they arrived, Theresa was visibly exhausted. My parents were anxious to come over to see her. They spent a short time making small talk. It was clear the weight of their daughter's fate was palpable. You could feel the sorrow and nervousness in the air. Prior to now, the tension was noticeable for other reasons, but for today, it was the weight of their guilt and desperation to make peace with their daughter.

Theresa was sad that her family would soon be feeling tremendous pain when she was gone, but hoped they would gain strength and courage to move forward by remembering her bravery and conviction. She did not shy away from her cancer, but rather analyzed its meaning, struggled with its meaning, and when she accepted its meaning, she could give everyone close to her the tools to overcome the sadness.

Theresa's strong will would give them strength as time passed, but for today, she was tired. Her face grew pale, her breathing labored. I could see the desire to comfort Mom and Dad was getting to be too much for her. She was trying to lessen their sorrow and perhaps help them face what was happening to their daughter, easing the blow that the miracle they prayed for would never be granted.

"You need to lie down." I motioned for Theresa to go upstairs to her room.

My head was throbbing from all the caffeine I had consumed that day just to be alert from my preceding sleepless night. Mom gave her a hug and watched as I escorted Theresa up the stairs.

"We'll see you tomorrow, okay?"

Riley squeezed his big wet nose against Theresa's hand as I laid her down on the bed. I could tell by the look on his face he didn't like what he was seeing. He wagged his stub of a tail when she said his name and looked up at me as if questioning me about what someone had done to her. She was frail and weak. Her body wilted into the thick, down blanket, and he, once again, kept guard at the foot of her bed as she dozed off to sleep.

My parents waited for me at the bottom of the stairs. Mom had previously suffered through breast and colon cancer, both extremely serious, but thankfully, doctors caught it in time.

"The miracle was wasted on me," she insisted.

I gave her a hug and walked them to their car. I wanted so badly to be there for them, but I started this quest to take care of my sister, and there was no room for distractions. I knew they were nervous about what would happen next. From that day forward, they came over every day without exception. Some days, they would sit downstairs with me while Theresa slept. Just their presence, perhaps, provided comfort and support.

I checked on Theresa to see if she needed anything. I handed her a red walkie-talkie and showed her how to use it. I strapped the matching one to my waistband and told her to call me if she needed anything.

She seemed eager to talk, so I sat on the edge of the bed, waiting for her to fall to pieces, but she didn't. She was strangely at peace, only seeming to become emotional when she talked about her kids. She worried she wouldn't be able to instill the tools to help them finish what she started for them. Christopher was doing great in school, and she hoped he could get through this. She was afraid he would want to take time off to be by her side when he found out the severity of her condition.

"You'll be right by their side," I insisted.

"There won't be time for that," she replied.

I meant spiritually; however, this didn't seem like the right time to clarify my comment. She told me this cancer reminded her of a game we used to play as kids. We called it "throwing shoes." It was a treacherous game; we armed ourselves before bed with all the shoes we could gather, and when the lights went out, each of us knelt on our twin bed across the room from the other, hurling our ammunition. The shoes would slam hard against the walls behind us, leaving scuff marks on the paint as we bobbed and weaved. Inevitably, one or both of us would wind up with a bruise or a welt by morning.

"I'm ready," she insisted. "I'm going to dodge this killer shoe for as long as I can."

We laughed about things we did together as kids. Swimming in the pool until all hours of the night; playing shark with my best friend, Lillian, until our eyes were red and blurry from the chlorine.

Without much warning, Theresa dozed off. At that moment, I held my breath so I could make sure I could hear hers. I felt that my compassion and willingness to give her the best shot at making time stand still would be awarded to her if I just gave it my all.

As the days passed, I jumped in the raft with her. We were connected, and I was committed to being on this voyage with her no matter where it took us. If I could just ride the ebb and flow of the waves with her, we could conquer this beast.

Her body was now home to a biliary drain along with a feeding tube. The biliary drain circumvented the excess bile past the obstruction from her liver, which seemed almost barbaric but a necessary evil. She emptied her own drain as if it was just another chore added to her daily routine. I offered many times to help her, but she insisted on handling it herself.

"This is disgusting," she said. "We both don't need to be tortured by this."

I knew she was trying to protect me from the corruption of the vile stench.

"This thing smells like rotten eggs." Like a broken record, she repeated the same verse.

She was soon becoming my hero. I don't mean in the sense of perfect or godlike. No one is ever without flaws. However, her desire to prevail over the hurdles in front of her made her a champion in my book. She faced each misstep and letdown in her life with such conviction, problem-solving her way through each minefield.

For now, we kept the feeding tube clean and clear until we needed it. Unable to eat any solid food due to the obstructions, she ate a blended diet. She made a makeshift papoose for her new additions, allowing them to go undetected beneath her clothing.

She had been home now for about a week. That morning when I emerged from the shower, she wasn't in her room. Nervously, I rushed downstairs, only to find her sitting at the kitchen table making some notes.

"I need to pick up the trust paperwork from the attorney today, and I probably should start deciding on funeral arrangements. I can't decide—bugs or fire."

The reality of what she was saying was something I didn't want to face right now. She had been such a big part of my formative past that made me who I am today. I was not ready to organize her departure, therefore, losing our past altogether. People make their funeral arrangements every day, but usually, it isn't when death is staring them in the face. I was not going to allow her to plan her own funeral, no matter how hard she pushed for it. I knew her best, and when that fateful day came, I would make sure to celebrate her life.

Theresa began smoking in her early twenties. It wasn't until her thirties she decided to quit. Tired of making excuses and trying to get back to a healthier self, she quit cold turkey. She knew her years of smoking were potentially the cause of her current condition. Yet, she didn't make excuses or try to reduce her culpability by asking, "Why me?" Remorse was for cheating spouses and underachievers, which she was neither.

I could see her mind-set changing, the distance between the life she had a few months back and the one she would now be living. She knew the survival curve dropped sharply once the doctor was unable to perform the Whipple. The survival rate past a year was about five percent. While remaining painfully realistic with herself, she left plenty of room for error.

My sister, Phyllis, made somewhat of a schedule to stop by most nights after work. Theresa designated her executor of the trust for the kids. Knowing people weren't coming to visit me, I made sure each visitor could have their private time with her.

Phyllis had a very polarized view on life; everything was either black or white, leaving no room for a grey area. She was incredibly smart, and when it came to her job as a professor, colleagues, and students either favored her or feared her, which was never an issue for her as long as they respected her.

Many nights, Phyllis and Theresa would talk about Theresa's wishes for Veronica and Christopher. She knew Phyllis was the best person for the task. Fearing her young children would stray off course once she was gone, Phyllis would make sure they stayed close to the plan Theresa laid out for them.

However, this evening, Theresa was so upset about Veronica. She barely came over and ignored most of Theresa's phone calls. Theresa wanted them to grow up so fast, not realizing that they were young and have always had her to count on. Accepting her departure was something Veronica was unwilling to accept. I knew she was silently yelling inside, *How could my mother do this to me!* That daily jab in the stomach that her mom was dying, and that there was nothing she could do about it, hurt.

She hoped her children would be resilient, able to finish growing up without her. Like most young adults, they hadn't gotten to the point where they appreciated their own lives and realized how their mom got them there. I think that comes with time, when you grow up and have your own children.

Theresa called me into the room to join the conversation. "She thinks she's punishing me. I want to spend as much time as I can with her; I need her to be there for Christopher. She doesn't understand how important this time is for us. She is so stubborn; I'll be dead before she figures this all out!"

Phyllis remarked, "She'll come around, just give her time."

"I don't have control over time. *That's* the problem."

Chapter 8

Theresa's birthday was approaching quickly, and I thought a party would be good for the family. I hoped everyone could come to terms with this vital, independent sister, daughter, mother, and friend in their lives who is still vibrant and full of life. Any major illness would usually transform a person, but her change seemed to grow her into a more awe-inspiring and committed person than ever before.

Three months came and went, and Theresa was still alive and fighting. She slept a lot more and the time between the extreme bouts of pain was less and less. She began her research into alternatives that might help her increase her energy while trying to slow down her cancer that had set up shop in her body. On the days when the pain was so persistent, time seemed to linger forever. On the rare days when her body gave her a reprieve from gripping pain, she challenged herself to do more.

Someone told her about Doctor Johanna Budwig, a German pharmacist who had a doctorate in chemistry and physics that had developed an anticancer diet in the 1950s.

An avid vegetarian, she based her research on that lifestyle. The core behind the idea was that by changing the fats in one's diet could kill cancer cells. The diet primarily consisted of cottage cheese and flaxseed, along with mainly fruits and vegetables while avoiding sugars and animal fats.

Theresa read through the material in the book, while I gathered the necessary supplies to start the plan. She embraced the alternative method, hoping to increase her strength. Although she hadn't eaten solid food in the last few months, she was remarkably satisfied with whatever liquid drinks that were sustaining her life. However, she continued to drop weight, something she knew would hasten her demise. I often caught myself saying how hungry I was, forgetting that everything she consumed had to fit through a straw.

"I'm hungry," she confessed.

"What type of shake do you want?"

"I'd kill for spaghetti and meatballs."

I grinned. "Okay, I'm on it, but it is going to resemble tomato soup."

She giggled as I cranked up the blender.

The next morning, I conjured up her first meal. She came down and stared at the concoction that sat in front of her on the kitchen table. I could see the overwhelming desire to vomit as she choked it down. I could only imagine the tremendous desire to make this work. As she grappled with the last bit, she lay her head down on the table.

"This is like Agent Orange," she declared. "This should be used to torture prisoners."

Over the next few weeks, she tried hard to stuff down the dreadful potion, but her body had a different plan in mind. It was fight or flight. With each bite, she closed her eyes and hoped it would stay down. Still, shortly after each try, her body would go into a wrathful expulsion of the contents she had just consumed.

She had a follow-up appointment with Doctor Reeves the next day. Knowing her cancer had a grim prognosis, she still looked forward to her visits with him. Throughout our time with Doctor Reeves, I always wondered how he managed to keep it all together, having such sick patients in his care, knowing full well death always wins. Theresa would have many private conversations with him over time, whether it was in his office or at her bedside when she was in the hospital for the many infections that would plague her throughout their relationship. Whatever they spoke about kept her strong and determined.

Margaret's house would become our spike camp, and my house the base camp. Between appointments or emergency tube clogs, we would take many trips to her place. Margaret had a room set up especially for Theresa. I slept most nights on the trundle bed in the office, sometimes sharing the bed with Theresa if she didn't want to be alone. Margaret's husband was spending a lot of time at his parents' home in Oregon, due to his father's failing health. So, we were like bachelorettes. Not as wild, but surely having a lot of fun. Each time we were together, made me appreciate what I had, and the most important thing was, we had each other.

Margaret's home would prove to be a stress reliever for me. I found myself able to relax and allow someone else to share the responsibilities with me. I would relinquish my driving duties to my big sister. A glass of wine or a margarita always seemed to be in order as well. Aside from that, it gave me a chance to once again bond with my sisters. Oftentimes, life gets in the way of sharing it with those to whom you should remain the closest. Our family was no exception.

"You both have given me the most valuable thing that life can offer. You gave me the freedom to laugh and love with the family I thought had become just a memory," Theresa said.

The next day, we checked in at the hospital, and they weighed her before going into the exam room. Margaret, Theresa, and I all glanced at the scale, hoping for no weight loss. Alas, we were disappointed. Another four pounds down. This once-chubby girl, who wished for a slimmer figure, now panicked at the thought of dropping an ounce. Doctor Reeves pulled up her last radiologic exam. While viewing the current CT scan images that illuminated on the computer screen, it showed that her cancer had raided multiple areas, making the diagnosis profoundly clear. The stomach stent and biliary drain wires resembled a freeway overpass, with lots of diversions.

Even though cancer had physically weakened her body, her spirit grew stronger with each visit. Her struggles and carefully planned life had buckled beneath her, but she welcomed the chance to continue this new life she was handed.

They spoke at length about chemotherapy treatment. Something she knew all too well would only prolong her life for a short time. Never having any intention to do treatment, she felt it necessary to ask his advice, not for herself but rather her children. Many of these cancer treatment centers focus their attention on the word "hope." With the severity of Theresa's condition, it only seemed like just another four-letter word.

"What are your thoughts?" she asked.

"I have always viewed the quality of life rather than the quantity of time. But, this is something you need to decide for yourself."

She trusted him with all her might and knew he would protect her until it was time for her to go. I usually gave her the space to have these frank conversations with him, but this time, I was present and not prepared for his answers. I was working so hard to keep her here, and these harsh realities only deflated my optimism.

I felt oddly anxious that time was not standing still for her. She was trying to figure out the game plan for the next few months of her life, nothing further than that. Weeks were quickly falling off the calendar and I worried that time was moving faster than I was ready for, like a car out of control rushing to the edge of a cliff. She was perhaps preparing her soul for the inevitable. I tried to welcome her questions, but it made me uneasy. Now, I felt naive, suddenly unwilling to face the fact she was leaving me soon, always somehow believing our time together would last forever.

They talked about a job offer with another hospital. Something she had hoped would come through for her only a short time ago. With that now out of her reach, she spoke with him about doing some consulting in her spare time. They discussed hospital business as if they worked together. I don't think she was searching for something to keep her mind busy, but rather she truly enjoyed the challenges of running a hospital.

Theresa was always an avid swimmer, and the thought of never getting in the water again seemed to bother her the most. She asked when the doctor might remove the feeding tube and perhaps if they could internalize the biliary drain.

They broached this option previously and now seemed like as good a time as any to inquire if it was still possible.

"I'll set you up with interventional radiology. They can make those arrangements and see if it will be a viable option."

The doctor had his nurse call down to the department to see if they could squeeze her in so we wouldn't have to make another long and tasking trip back. Not long after the nurse emerges.

"They can see you at three p.m. today."

Margaret picked us up outside the hospital, and we went for a little retail therapy and lunch between appointments. To conserve her strength, I would get a wheelchair wherever we went. By now, Theresa had become a connoisseur of which restaurants had the best soups without chunks.

I began carrying a small strainer with me in my purse after we encountered an unfortunate soup chunk incident. She opted for some tomato soup on one of our lunch outings, which proved disastrous. As she swallowed a small spoonful of soup, the color in her face drained. A tomato chunk had made its way down her throat, and, without warning, she leaned her head forward over the bowl and threw it all back up. A stream of hot tomato soup and chunky bits of liquid came from both her mouth and her nostrils. Perhaps throwing up through her nose was a strong enough warning that she needed to be that careful, so we opted to always strain everything ourselves from that point forward.

The outdoor mall was paved with cobblestone. I picked up the pace to ease the bumpiness, leaving Margaret to run behind with her short little legs, trying to keep up with my long stride. Theresa looked back, laughing hysterically.

"She can't keep up!" she shrieked.

The airstream from the wheelchair ride was whipping through her hair. Theresa clasped her jacket closed to keep the wind off her chest. She held her arms in tight and laughed as I raced down the sidewalk.

When we reached the restaurant, I was out of breath. I leaned over, putting my hands on my knees, trying to catch my breath as we cackled wildly. Our intense dash made me feel vibrant and happy.

"I'm having a mojito," I proclaimed. "It's five o'clock somewhere."

Margaret finally reached us. She had given up trying to catch us, mostly because she was laughing so hard. Her eyes were watering, and her cheeks were rosy from the sprint.

"Are you trying to give your big sis a heart attack?"

It seemed almost cruel that we were having such a great time, all the while knowing it would end sooner rather than later. I found myself torn between joy and sadness for having such pleasure and pain, all in the same instance.

Everyone handles their worst fear in their own way. My sister chose laughter. Humor was her savior. We drew strength from her contagious personality that allowed us to fill our days with love and happiness.

In the afternoon, we headed back to the hospital for her appointment with interventional radiology. The doctor conceded that while it was possible to do the procedure, the biliary stent and the duodenal stent were in a battle for space, making internalizing the drain almost impossible without constant complications. Her biliary drain was perpetually clogging, putting her at a higher risk for infection. The nauseousness and vomiting that occurred, if she tried to eat anything thicker than a shake, were arduous, so the duodenal stent was a must, proving the point that the dual stenting wouldn't support the process.

Although Doctor Reeves was willing to remove the surgically implanted feeding tube, I was apprehensive about it. My feeling was that if she had any hopes of keeping weight on and building up her strength, she should take advantage of it. On the drive home, I talked to Theresa about utilizing the feeding tube.

"I think you should take advantage of this. It will give you your daily calories and, hopefully, increase your energy."

Theresa was apprehensive, but willing to listen to my argument. "I just don't want to be a patient. I feel like I'm giving in, using the feeding tube."

I responded, "No, you are fighting with all the tools at your disposal."

All these decisions were critical to Theresa's succeeding or failing. Her goal was to win and therefore, at this juncture, she knew I was making sense. I tried to prepare her for each new turn of events as it presented itself. Initially, I had started this mission to make her as content as possible, but then a fight within me came alive. I was in the brutal struggle with her, grasping at every tool that would give her more time.

All I could see now was the past she needed to leave behind, the memories, the victories, and losses. I needed her to be in the present; I would rally for the things I knew were best for her, all the while allowing her to keep her independence intact, hoping to appeal to her intelligence.

We needed to no longer fear new things, but rather, embrace them with open arms.

When we arrived home, Riley met us, gave her a kiss, and walked closer to her side as I escorted Theresa up the stairs to lie down. He would prove to give her endless support as her cancer progressed. I brought him a toy from the local pet store, which he soon came to expect when we returned. Theresa would laugh out loud, as he immersed his big block-shaped head into my overnight bag, searching for his gift.

Theresa was resilient; she was a fighter; her objective was to prevail. She would do whatever needed to be done to stay one step ahead. From that point forward, using the feeding tube would be a godsend. I don't think she had one minute where she felt it wasn't worth the time she had to spend hitched to that machine. She realized then that every second she would waste worrying about how to stay alive or about her cancer growing inside her would only be forfeiting precious time.

Mom and Dad came by for a visit when we returned, but Theresa was weak and exhausted from the trip, so I told them she was too drained to come down.

Mom proclaimed, "I'm going up." She looked back at Dad, who struggled to follow. "You're coming, too?" she remarked.

"Yes, why? You don't think the stairs will hold us both?" Dad grinned as he grasped the banister tightly to keep his balance.

Theresa heard my parents coming up the stairs and got out of bed to greet them at the top. "I would've come down," she insisted.

Theresa's strength would remain unwavering to those around her. Her ability to accept her fate made everyone at ease. Even as the bad days seemed to outweigh the good, I often wondered how she did it. I spent every waking moment with her except while sleeping, and she never seemed to veer from that uplifting spirit.

She had intertwined herself into the morality of life and death, and, in the grand scheme, what her place would be. She displayed such conviction, knowing she was going to live her life to the fullest and to allow herself to embrace death whenever that time would come.

When someone is looking death in the face, somehow, the people around them begin to view them as some kind of saint...or someone to pity. Yet, she didn't play into that notion; rather, she knew the deck was stacked against her and every day that she woke up was a blessing. She was realistic in her views and sensed there was a reason she was given this time.

I didn't need to search far as to why she embraced her new unchartered life; it was the desire to make sure her children would be equipped to live life without her, which gave her the strength to push through the tidal waves of pain and suffering. She never took her time with everyone for granted. She confronted the meaning of life, realizing that death would come to all of us at some point. She was going to take advantage of every moment, not allowing any time she had remaining feeling sorry for herself. She wanted to right some wrongs, laugh, and cry along with family and friends until her judgment day was upon her.

Chapter 9

That evening, I drove Theresa to the airport to pick up Christopher; it was spring break. This would be her time to give him the entire news about her condition. From the start, she wanted him to realize his mother was dying, and their time together was essential. Her biggest fear was that he would be blindsided, wandering aimlessly, like an emotional cripple. She wanted to guide him through the process while giving him the strength to continue with his life and the goals she had worked so hard for him to attain. College was the most important goal to her, and not finishing wasn't an option. She had carefully planned his future, and her death was not going to change the course of all her hard work, or more importantly, his.

Theresa escorted Christopher up the stairs to her room and broke the news to him. He remained calm, as his eyes filled with water. The look on his face was as if the ground was crumbling below him. He tried asking a few questions, but the knot in his throat was holding him back. Trying to console his mom, while grasping for an explanation, was just too much. He knew her condition wasn't good, but this was a punch right in the guts.

"We can go over the details at another time," she continued. "This is a lot to take in all at once."

Having spent the better part of the evening hugging and holding her young son in her arms, she was becoming markedly weaker. She finally fell fast asleep. I motioned for him to come downstairs with me. This was, perhaps, one of the most difficult conversations I would expect to have in my lifetime. I tried hard to stay strong, consoling him, all the while knowing I, too, was losing such an important person in my life.

We sat at the kitchen table, talking. He asked several questions, but they all led back to the same outcome. It was a tough conversation. I wanted to be as honest with him as possible, while helping him cherish the remaining time he would have with her.

He spoke about friends who had family members that had gone through a cancer scare, remarking about reassuring outcomes they had shared. I knew he was only grasping for a hint of hope for his mom, but I held to Theresa's standard of honesty.

"Christopher, there are some cancers that are treatable, and some that are not. This one is not. The surgery was her best hope for more time, but that was unsuccessful."

I sensed the hole the news left in his heart. There aren't many comforting words to express when death is imminent. How do you tell someone's son there is no optimistic outcome for his mother, and that my only hope for him would be to try to enjoy his remaining time with her?

It was very sad. She and he had planned this life for him, and now, she would be taken away from him at perhaps the most critical part. He wanted to spend as much time with her as possible, but knew if he honored her wishes, he would be away at college for most of her final days.

Later that week, Theresa told me about a man she had dated some time back. He was a successful businessman who kept a similar grueling schedule, making it difficult to connect.

"David wants to come out and see me," she said. "He wants to try to rekindle our relationship."

She had put off letting him come out for some time, fearing her appearance might be shocking. Her devotion to her appearance was the same as her work ethic—impeccably organized and always putting her best effort into both. She hadn't been sporting those wigs she loved so much, so I made her an appointment to get her hair done. Her mousy brown ponytail would not be acceptable. Looking refreshed and feeling confident, she welcomed the visit.

Matt took Riley for a walk, so I left the house, too, to give them some time alone. When we returned, we decided to tackle the task of putting up the party tent I had bought for Theresa's birthday bash. She sat outside on a beach chair, staring into the sunlight, smiling, knowing this was all for her, and almost certain this would be her last birthday.

Later, she told me David wanted to whisk her away on a trip or have her come to stay with him for a bit. She graciously declined, knowing that wasn't possible. He, of all her gentlemen callers, was successful and could afford to spoil her. It made me sad for her. Finally, someone wanted to take care of her needs and give her that long, overdue rest.

"I just wanted someone to love me and make me feel special," she said. "Not because they needed something from me, but because they truly wanted to spend time with me."

"I miss my life. It wasn't great; it wasn't spectacular, but it suited me. I was finding me, finally. I always seem to want what I can't have, and I will breathe my last breath wanting it. I wanted to feel like a desired woman, not just a boss or a mom. I was exploring that, and I liked it. It was hard at first, finding normal. Eventually, I found me a few good ones."

— From Theresa's Journal

A master at disguising her drains, she, too, almost forgot they were there at times. However, her body had become noticeably different, and she was painfully mindful that no one would be able to welcome a physical relationship with her in her frail condition. One chapter of her life seemed to be ending. From that point forward, she settled for harmless flirting and perhaps some intimate hand-holding.

Derek became more and more prominent in her life. Most weekends he came out and stayed, leaving late Sunday evening. I tried hard not to let it bother me, but with each visit, it became more and more evident that she was still managing his life for him. He hovered over her, making it difficult to attend to her needs.

I questioned her many times about their connection. She insisted until her last dying breath that their relationship ended because they took each other for granted. Still, I trusted my instincts more than words. I am a firm believer of having a strong sense of control over my world. This, I would soon realize, she lacked. There are times when I am wrong, but I never doubt my gut. This situation would be no different. She had a bad picker when it came to men, making her vulnerable to the weak-willed.

We spoke on many occasions about her life. She believed life was about choices, and she had to find the right ones for herself through this passage. In my heart of hearts, I think Derek knew something about her, something private that she wanted kept secret.

The birthday party was uplifting for Theresa, but mostly for all of us.

"No mushy cards," she insisted.

In truth, her cancer helped fix our fragmented family. However, as the day continued, there was no sign of Veronica. I could see it bothered Theresa that she hadn't come. It was now a few hours into the day and still there was no word. Noticing his mother's disappointment, Christopher feverishly tried calling her. After some time, he emerged, enraged with a story that she was making a photo quilt for Theresa.

"Why didn't she do it before the party?" he barked. "She is so selfish."

Theresa wanted to spend as much time with her children, but Veronica's defiance would only continue to get in the way of that dream. Exhausted, she went to lie down, and the crowd began to fade. She had an amazing day, apart from her missing daughter. That was the day she promised herself to accept the life she had now, and if that meant her daughter was going to be absent, she had to let the sorrow go and focus her energy on herself and those who chose to be around.

Later that evening, while Theresa was barely awake, Veronica and Clark strolled over to the house, with photo blanket in hand. Theresa smiled and accepted the gift, but I could tell by her expression that she felt the gesture was empty. Deep down, I think Veronica resented her mother for making amends with her parents and the sisterhood we shared. However, verbalizing that would just seem petty, and, therefore, she chose to punish her mother by her absence.

Driving down to see the oncologist the next morning was difficult for Theresa. She was confident about her decision not to do chemotherapy, but felt it only seemed logical to meet with the doctors about possible alternatives to her care. Up to this point, she hadn't taken any pain medication. Always mindful that the drugs would alter her awareness, she worried that would hinder her thoughts. Yet, as her cancer grew and her pain heightened, it became apparent she needed to take something. If not for the pain, then for her sanity.

Trying hard not to cave into the mental and physical stress she was feeling that morning, she searched for a Bruno Mars song to take her mind off what lay ahead. She was clearly in a lot of pain, and the heaviness of the appointment was weighing on her mind. Normally, she stayed awake on our drives to be my navigator, but the pain was overwhelmingly evident. I grabbed a pillow from the back seat so she could lean her head against the car window, and she finally dozed off. Now down forty pounds from her chubby frame, the bed was hurting her when she would lie down. With the muscle wasting and weight loss, every part of her body felt the stitching of the mattress.

When we arrived at Margaret's house, she woke up, startled, and quickly jumped from the car. She paused for a moment on the front lawn. With a flushed face, she was nauseated, unable to get the feeling to pass. As Margaret opened the door, she rushed to the bathroom to throw up. Emerging a few moments later, she lay curled up on the couch.

"I'm nervous," she said. "I'm not sure why, but this appointment is really getting to me."

She seemed sluggish for most of the day while she awaited our departure to the appointment, apparently content to sleep through the morning. However, I knew she was hiding; hiding from the reality that she would have to acknowledge her illness one more time.

The oncology department felt quite sterile. The room was absent of any character, both decoratively and spiritually. The patients in the waiting area sat quietly with their loved ones. Some were knocking on death's door, while others seemed healthy. The nurse weighed her in, something she would grow to dread with every appointment. We sat in a small exam room, side-by-side, and awaited the doctor's arrival. A thin Asian man, wearing a mask, entered the room, which seemed to lower the comfort level that much more.

"Excuse my appearance," he said. "I'm getting over a cold."

Without any warm-up, he spoke bluntly about her condition. "Using the Kaplan-Meier survival estimator, you have three to six months, best-case scenario," he stated.

Three months had already passed since her initial diagnosis, so was it three more or six? He had just reduced her life expectancy to a mathematical calculation. Anything after that seemed trivial. He said the only treatment that she could undergo for her aggressive cancer would be very difficult and would only add on a few months, at best.

Acknowledging her job, he remarked, "Most people that have been in the medical field for any time don't opt for that treatment. I guess they are acutely aware of the outcome."

She remained stoic in the appointment, recalling Doctor Reeves said she might make it to Christmas. This doctor just chopped six months out of the equation. He suggested enrolling her in palliative care, which will slowly transform into hospice. He prescribed her some medication for both the pain and nausea and had the nurse arrange for a service near us.

"The palliative team will take care of any additional needs." He handed her a prescription. "But, for now, this should help you get through the next few days."

We went downstairs to the pharmacy. Theresa lay down on an oversized chair and began to cry. "What are my kids going to do?"

At that moment, I realized there was no comforting response to the burden that had just been lowered on top of her. Up until that point, she was aware that her past life had ended and a new version was in place. But, this doctor had now, single-handedly, shortened the end of the story and collapsed Theresa's personal identity along with it.

Having spent the better part of that evening lying on the couch sleeping, she awoke back to her bubbly self. Perhaps the anti-nausea medication gave her the much-needed break from the stomach-churning torment. In any event, she had put oncology behind her, and while the news was upsetting, it wasn't shocking.

"I knew all these answers, but it just becomes more real each time someone reminds me that my life will be ending soon."

She felt her life was slipping away faster than she could take care of what she thought was important. We tried to console her, but mostly listened. Her strength still amazed me. I felt so lost for words; I couldn't imagine how she was feeling. I could only selfishly feel my own emotions.

"This was my meltdown day," she joked. "Tomorrow will be better."

The bulk of the rest of the week we met with the palliative staff that would manage her care from this point forward. However, Doctor Reeves would always stay at the forefront of her care. He had scheduled her for a dilation stent from the stomach to the small intestine. Hopefully, this would broaden her food options.

The palliative administrator would be coming to evaluate Theresa and inform us what we could expect going forward. The morning ticked by slowly as we awaited his arrival. I know she viewed each new addition to her care as just another confirmation the end was nearing.

When Paul arrived, he was informative and uplifting. He explained that cancer feeds off the person, therefore causing the weight loss and giving a means for it to grow. He educated her on the need to keep her strength up to give her longevity. She finally felt like someone other than Doctor Reeves was giving her positive thoughts about the remaining time she would have.

"Wouldn't you rather feel robust to go out and enjoy the things you love, than have to stay in bed because of weakness and overwhelming pain?"

He made her feel like she had their support.

"It might take a little fine-tuning, but we'll get you there," he continued. "We want you to wake up and say, 'I can do this. I have the strength to do the things I love.'

"I'm going to set you up with the two Carlys. One will be your nurse, and the other your social worker."

Theresa was excited and confident her new team would be an asset to her. Later that afternoon, they both arrived. Their visit was lengthy, and she tired quickly. Nurse Carly addressed some of my questions and made me a bit more at ease moving forward. Up until this point, it was manageable, but I knew a time would come when I might need someone I could lean on with my concerns.

Theresa had done some research and felt the plant-based feeding would be the best option for her, providing her with vitality to support her already compromised immune system, all the while giving the body the nourishment and controlling the pancreatic hormone insulin, which was vital to her overall health. Carly arranged for a wheelchair, a mattress topper, and the feeding tube supplementation.

Her social worker was laid-back and easy to talk to. She spoke at length with Theresa, while Carly finished up her evaluation. Initially, Theresa didn't feel it was necessary to have a social worker. What did she need her for? However, as they spoke, calmness came over her, and she realized she would not only be there for her, but more importantly, for her children.

Later that evening, I picked up Christopher from his father's house and brought him over to spend some time with his mother before he went back to college. He asked if he could spend the night. I made a makeshift bed on the floor with an air mattress and left them to talk. He is an amazing person; his relaxed attitude and sense of humor never failed to entertain his mother.

Tomorrow was her birthday, and her driver's license was expiring. While she hadn't driven in over three months, nor would she probably ever drive again, she was unwilling to give up that luxury. Insistent that we go to the DMV, Christopher decided to take her for the outing.

The next morning, I heard her stirring in the kitchen, so I proceeded downstairs to see if they needed anything before they left. Theresa was in a cold sweat, and her face was pasty. She held onto the counter for support as she tried to get water from the refrigerator. I escorted her to the couch.

"You aren't going anywhere. I will go get the appointment number and come back to get you."

Christopher stood quietly, but the nervous look on his face said it all.

"It's okay," I assured him. "Just keep her company while I'm gone."

An hour in line, the woman made an exception to give me the number. I ran back to the house and grabbed Theresa to make the appointment time. We no sooner got in the door and her number was called. She was in so much pain she could barely get through the eye test and photo. All I could think was, *I hope she'll still be alive by the time we get her driver's license in the mail.* What a terrible thought, but realistic, considering her current condition.

When we returned, I got her settled into bed, and then I went into my bedroom to hide. I stood in my closet, crying, hoping to gain my composure. I just kept telling myself, "It'll be okay." It seemed like the harder I tried to keep her here, the harder her cancer fought back.

Riley came to console me. He knew I was afraid; afraid I would let my sister down with my weakness. I felt like she was in front of a firing squad, dodging the deadly bullet that would someday take her from us. He looked up at me and sighed his Riley sigh. I leaned down and gave him a hug, holding his face against mine. That made me cry harder, knowing he, too, was feeling my sadness.

Christopher was leaving for school this evening. He stopped by to spend some time with his mom. Around eight-thirty, his dad texted and said he was on his way. Theresa got up and gave him a big hug. As her tiny body sunk into his embrace, she tried hard to keep it together, knowing this might be the last time she would see her son.

"Be good, do good in school. Make sure you make something of yourself," she instructed him.

Chapter 10

The next morning, she received a telephone call, answering the cloud of doubt that she might not be able to feed enough. Interventional radiology had an opening to place the dilation stent and internalize the biliary drain. She was excited, but anxious, hoping this would provide her with an added means of feeding. I traversed through the dreadful afternoon traffic, making it to Margaret's house late in the evening.

In the early-morning hours, we headed to the hospital. After an hour or so in surgery, the doctor emerged. She did well. The stent was placed nicely, and now it was a waiting game to see if she could tolerate it. When we were finally able to see her in recovery, she was clearly in a lot of pain and suffering. They contacted the anesthesiologist to come down to prescribe some pain medication. Perplexing, however, the doctor refused to provide the drugs. The nurse came in mortified, knowing Theresa would not be able to get through the next hour, let alone the night, without medication.

The nurse could clearly see the aggravation on my face. She, too, was annoyed. I verbalized my anger to her, and she nodded in agreement. After much confusion, she decided to page Doctor Reeves.

Theresa was nauseated and in severe pain. The green hue that was now masking her face was a clear indication she was destined to throw up. Nervously, her young nurse handed her a Styrofoam cup. Without hesitation, I grabbed a much-needed pink basin from the supply cart outside her door. The nurse watched in amazement as she filled up more than half the bucket.

She was withering from the ravenous barfing, barely able to keep her body upright against the pillow. She shivered uncontrollably as her nurse tried to bundle her with warm blankets. I held her hand beneath the blankets, consoling her, hoping to calm her.

Shortly after Doctor Reeves arrived, realizing her distressing condition, he quickly rattled off orders to the nurse, hoping to relieve Theresa's symptoms rapidly. Grimacing at the fact that they were even giving her an issue, he tried to distract her with good news, telling her the stent was in a perfect position. Now they just needed to wait to see if her body could bear it.

"I'll give you whatever you need," he said. "Do not hesitate to have them page me if you have any problems."

By this point, the pain was so out of control that he decided to admit her for the night. After a long, arduous day, she finally got comfortable in a room and could sleep. The next morning, my phone was blowing up with multiple texts from her.

Where are you guys?

I want to get out of here.

When Margaret and I arrived, she was perched on the edge of the bed in her hospital gown.

"The nurse can't find my clothes," she stated. "Where'd you guys put them?"

We looked at each other, clueless, our feet glued to the floor. We ran out of the house so fast, I forgot to grab her bag. I could feel a grin overriding my face. "I left it at the house."

"So, what am I going to wear out of here?" She tried to flog us with her anger, which made us both giggle even more.

"Here, wear my sweatshirt. I have a T-shirt on underneath." I removed my pullover and handed it to her.

Flailing her arms, she shook her finger at us. "Yeah, and pants. What do I do for pants? Wear my little boy-short undies?"

By this point, she was enraged with us, and her gestures were making it even that much more comical. I caught the eye of a male nurse walking down the hall.

"Excuse me. Excuse me. Is there any way I can get my sister some pants to wear home? We forgot her clothes."

He looked at me for a split second, confused about the question. He poked his head in the room to see why all the excitement. Theresa reacted to his presence.

"Yeah, my sisters didn't bring me clothes!"

He realized there was no crisis and told her he'd be right back. He emerged in a few short minutes with a package of red and black checkered boxer shorts. "Will this work?"

Realizing how silly the whole thing was, she gave him a huge smile. "Perfect. Now I'll only look like one of the drunks that barf all over their clothes in the emergency room."

Margaret and I were now in full hysterics. She slipped the boxers on over her underwear and put my sweatshirt on over the hospital gown. I gave her the thumbs-up when she turned back around.

"I'm going to get you back for this," she promised.

Somehow, through all the fun, she forgot about the pain and nausea. Margaret fetched the car and waited for us out front in the getaway vehicle. I made sure we had our pink bucket in hand, as we headed down to the loading area. Theresa handled the drive back to Margaret's house okay, but the nausea was still intolerable, no matter how much Zofran she took. She went into the bathroom and leaned over the toilet bowl. With intense vigor, she vomited so much I thought she was going to turn herself inside out.

As time passed, her body allowed her to relax. The three of us sat outside in the warm sun, laughing about the morning and talking about the upcoming wedding of Margaret's daughter. Desperately trying to figure out how she would do her hair, she asked our opinion about her choices.

"Let me show you both what I was thinking," she said. "I bought a few hairpieces."

Theresa and I glanced at each other, knowing whatever she was going to show us would surely not be trendy. Margaret was a bit of an old-fashioned girl, nine years my senior, with a habit of having some very questionable taste when it came to hairdos. She emerged from the house with this bird nest-like hairpiece tacked to the top of her head.

Without hesitation, Theresa blurted out, "You're kidding, right? That thing is hideous."

I chimed in, "Camille will kill you if you show up with that thing on your head."

Margaret was quite a jokester at times, so I thought that maybe she was pulling our leg. "I just have to fix it around my own hair. I'm just showing you the color." She twirled around so we could see the back.

Theresa stood to get a closer look. "Oh, Lord, Margaret... Color is the *least* of your problems." She reached up to feel the texture. "This thing is a bundle of hay. Do *not* embarrass us. If you are going to wear a clip-in, at least let's go to my wig place."

Worried Margaret would settle in with her wiglet find, Theresa insisted we immediately go shopping. "You guys hungry? I feel like soup."

She petitioned that we go to the Pizza Kitchen. I found her choice surprising because she cannot eat anything except soup. I think that maybe she just wanted to smell the food. When we got there, she decided on the tortilla soup. We had the waitress water it down and I strained out the chunks. Theresa nibbled on a piece of sourdough bread; not seeming to worry it might get stuck in the stent. Then she took a sip of my mojito, smiling as if she were doing something wild and uninhibited.

Afterward, we went to Bebo's Beauty Supply, one of Theresa's stomping grounds. We laughed in the store like kids, trying on unsuitable wigs. I cracked up, knowing full well Margaret wouldn't wear a wig nor would she look normal in it. I put on a long, bleach-blond Lady Godiva wig with a side ponytail. Strangely enough, it looked good.

"All I need is a horse," I proclaimed.

Our cousin, Jack, from New York was in town visiting for a few days. We hadn't seen him since we were kids. Mom had a luncheon planned. Meatballs and pasta ... What else?

Theresa was feeling the best she had in months. She was dressed super cute with her low-rise jeans and sparkle black crystal belt. I thought her attitude mostly was what made her so adorable. She embraced her new thinner self with open arms. She knew she couldn't change what brought her to this place, but she was going to enjoy how she felt in the moment. She was face-to-face with death, yet still found the strength to get up and appreciate who was looking back at her in the mirror.

Jack was no stranger to heartbreak, losing two of the most important people in his life at a very young age. His father died in his early fifties from liver cancer, and his mom died not long after that, I think from a broken heart. I couldn't help but think of Christopher at that time. He, too, would soon be feeling that pain. Hopefully, he would be able to move forward with his life, as Jack seemed to have done so successfully.

The next morning, Theresa told me she had been itching uncontrollably and her mid-back was in a tremendous spasm. I suggested we call Doctor Reeves's office to see if we could get in to see him. He arranged for us to see the interventional radiologist. Concerned about the itching, they ordered lab tests to check her bilirubin numbers.

The back spasms were intense. I rubbed her back while we waited. The doctor arrived a short time later, expressing that her bilirubin was fine, but her liver function test was much higher than previously tested.

"I don't think your body is tolerating the internalized drain." He shook his head. "I'm really sorry. I need to reverse it."

She was disappointed, hoping to be able to go in the pool or just take a normal shower without having to cover herself like a mummy in plastic wrap. She reached out her hand to touch his. "It's okay. You tried." I knew she was so disappointed, but made light of it, hoping not to make him feel bad.

I was having a wedding shower for Camille that coming weekend. With all the back-and-forth to the hospital, I opted to have it catered in case I ran short on time. We stopped at the craft store to pick up some decorations. Margaret forgot her car keys and had to run back inside.

Out of nowhere, Theresa said, "Am I going to live with you forever?"

Without skipping a beat, I answered, "Of course, unless you have a better plan."

I could see the tears spilling down her face as she continued to stare forward. "No, I'm just having so much fun; I don't want to be anywhere else."

I couldn't help but wonder where this was coming from. One minute we were shopping and laughing, and the next, she was wondering if I were going to send her away for someone else to take care of her.

That night, I called Matt and told him the story. He always has a way of putting things into the proper perspective. "It's like an airline stewardess on a bumpy plane ride. If she stays calm, so do the passengers. She's just drawing strength from you, making sure you're confident and not afraid about what is to come."

I texted the rest of the family her medical update. I took her to every appointment and I wouldn't have wanted it any other way. I became very possessive over her care. The other siblings offered, but they all worked, and therefore, Margaret and I were it.

It bothered me sometimes, not for myself, but for Theresa. She never said anything, but I often wondered if it bothered her. For me, when it was all said and done, I was going to have those precious days or months with my sister, and they were not. Memories that could never be erased. My time with Margaret became very special to me as well. Our difference in age seemed to have us at different stages in life, but this built a bond that could never be broken.

That morning, we were back at the hospital for the drain reversal. The procedure was short, and they called us in to see Theresa. Once again, she was in tremendous pain and extremely nauseated. A young, female anesthesiologist stopped by and told us everything went well. She gave Theresa a bit more medication for nausea.

"I'll give her half the dose and see how she does. If she needs more, I'll be right here."

A far cry from the last anesthesiologist she had the previous week. The interventional radiologist stopped by to discharge her. He expressed concern that there was "gunk," as he called it, in the area between the stomach and the small intestine that he cleared out. The sourdough morsel she had a few days prior come to mind. He showed us on the scan how the biliary drain and the dilation stent were competing in such a tight space.

"It is tight," he said. "But, I think it will be okay."

He told us to keep an eye out for excessive bile buildup in the external bag, which would be an indication of a clogged biliary drain. If I couldn't clear it, I would have to inject the bile back into her body via the feeding tube. How intricate our body is, yet so simple that everything runs together. He said there had been cases where patients must drink the bile, but he hasn't had a patient that had to do that in his career. The thought of that alone would make a healthy person vomit. The stench from the bile bag fell somewhere between feces and bad trash. I could only think no sane person could gag that down.

Theresa was prone to infection, so we stayed at Margaret's house for the next few days, allowing her to rest and, hopefully, avoid a return trip to the hospital. The drive down was getting increasingly more difficult, and she needed to reserve her strength. The first few days, she battled nausea, vomiting, and unrelenting pain. I heard the rushing of the fluid in the toilet as she threw up. All I could do was stand at the door with a cold washcloth.

"You okay?" I asked.

"Yeah, I am now." She retreated to the bedroom with the trash can under her arm in case she couldn't make it to the bathroom in time.

By the third day, she was weak, but much better, despite the torment her body had just endured. Margaret and I were sitting outside talking on the patio when she emerged. Not long after her arrival, a giant grasshopper was stalking me. It hopped closer, toying with my terror. I jumped up on the patio chair, trying to avoid it leaping on my leg. Theresa and Margaret laughed as they watched me keep a close eye on the leggy bug. I think I could walk on water if a grasshopper were after me.

I got Theresa a protein drink so she could take some pain medication, knowing full well if she doesn't have something in her stomach, she will throw the pill right up, not giving her any pain relief. She decided to go back to bed. After some time, I checked on her, and she was fast asleep, so I decided to take a shower to wash off the events of the day. I poked my head in her room once again. Now she was very white with a greenish tint; she looked gravely ill. She felt my presence and opened her eyes.

"Everything okay?" I asked.

"Yeah, good, just tired."

Margaret and her husband, Hank, were going to a co-ed shower for their daughter tomorrow. "Let me give you a facial," I insisted. "You'll be stunning."

Theresa chimed in from the other room. "Let her do it, but don't talk when she puts it on. She'll get it on your teeth." Something she had experienced on several occasions.

With some minor coaxing, I placed a clay mask on her, which turned khaki green rapidly. I could see her uneasiness, especially since her husband was laughing about her light avocado complexion.

I poked my head in Theresa's room. "You want one, too?"

"Not tonight. I'm green enough."

She was shivering, so I covered her with an extra blanket. A moment later, she jumped up from the bed and rushed into the bathroom. The vomiting had given way to violent diarrhea.

I realized her condition was worsening, and I knew a hospital visit was soon.

"I'm in total agony," she said. "I think I need to go to the hospital."

I gave her a confirming nod. "Okay, let's go."

I walked out and gave Margaret the news. With the mask covering her face, she was barely able to make an expression. She thought I was kidding with her at first.

"I'm serious," I insisted. "We need to go."

A minute later, she emerged, mask gone and keys in hand. Theresa sat quietly with her eyes closed as Margaret took the necessary shortcuts to get us to the hospital quicker. Theresa's eyes only widened when a beam of light crossed her eyelids from the oncoming traffic.

She needed IV fluids to avoid dehydration, which had plagued her many times from the constant vomiting cycles. We went through the emergency room, as Doctor Reeves had told us if it was after regular office hours. The emergency room doctor, who consulted with one of Doctor Reeves's colleagues, greeted us. They decided to order a CT scan and lab tests.

Margaret and I sat on a footstool, wrapped in blankets, trying to stay warm in the frigid surroundings. As the air blasted from the vent above us, we covered our heads with towels to keep warm. Meanwhile, Theresa lay still and quiet, wrapped up tightly, trying to take her mind off her symptoms. The doctor ordered Dilaudid for the pain and some nausea medication, barely giving her any relief.

After several hours in the emergency room bay, they finally admitted her. It was five o'clock in the morning, and I was beginning to feel the effects of no sleep. I attempted to read a magazine while Margaret called her husband, but even that was taxing. I set it aside and leaned over, putting my head in my hands to gather some vigor.

Over the next few hours, Theresa's color seemed to return and the excruciating pain had subsided. The doctor on call for Doctor Reeves arrived shortly after, revealing that the CT scan had revealed a liver abscess. Between her bouts of consciousness, she spoke with the doctor about the results and asked if Doctor Reeves knew her condition.

She would need to stay in the hospital for a few days, at least. "Doctor Reeves will be in to see you tomorrow and discuss the treatment plan," he said. "It is a good thing you came in when you did."

Luckily, the abscess responded well to the IV antibiotics, and within a week, Doctor Reeves released her from the hospital. Revitalized and refreshed, we were finally able to go back home. The spitefulness of a terminal illness is the desire to cram as much in a day as possible—without the energy to back it up. But, for now, Theresa was feeling amazing. Perhaps the abscess had been hiding for some time, causing her diminishing condition.

Her courage and dynamism were back. The last month or so consisted of setback after setback. I blasted God for not giving my sister a break just this once. She was battling an unrelenting illness while we held her hand through the process.

I tried so hard to confront my feelings, not to let my fear of losing her hold me back from enjoying my time with her. However, it was difficult, trying to hold onto hope that somehow a divine spirit was watching over her and giving her strength to continue.

That morning, the caterers arrived to set up for Camille's bridal shower. Theresa's weight loss had left her with few clothes that fit, so I ran out quickly to find something cute for her to wear. She offered to help me organize the games we had scheduled and sat cutting out colorful genitalia for the "pin the penis on the hot guy." Shocked by Theresa's appearance was written all over the guests' faces.

I marveled at how she bounced back. She always thrived when challenged, and this was no different. I had serious doubts most people could be as resilient as she was. She'd been up, she'd been down, but she *never* gave in without a fight, and her cancer would not receive special treatment.

That Sunday, Theresa went to Easter Mass with Mom. The church was crowded. They sat together on folding chairs in the back. There had been a long span in her life where she didn't attend Mass at all. We were raised devout Catholics; however, none of us attended church except for holidays and funerals. I think what brought her to church that day was the desire to make Mom happy. Or, perhaps because my parents had always believed if you pray, God will answer. In Theresa's mind, He did answer. She would soon be gone from this earth, and whatever was waiting for her in the afterlife, she was slowly accepting.

Deep inside all of us, I believe we have some perception that prayer will somehow change our life's course. Nevertheless, Theresa didn't buy into that notion; of all people, throughout her life, she had unrelenting determination. Yet, she did not fool herself into believing she could reverse her condition with prayer. Rather, she prayed for God to give her the strength to find peace in what was to come.

"I feel myself slipping away some days. Not even sleep gives me peace. I wonder if this is how it is supposed to be. I can't tell them I'm scared to think what it will be like without them. Will my children still laugh and stay close? I hope so. I have no words to express the fear I have. But, then, I think when the fear stops, I will stop fighting. I talked a lot to God today, and I didn't feel fear."
— From Theresa's Journal

That evening, we attempted to use the feeding tube. She did not welcome the feeding tube at first. She always reminded me of what the nurse had told her; her cancer was thriving off her calories, which, to her, made this a double-edged sword. The feeding process was slow, and to get in the adequate calories, she would need to spend up to eight hours captive to the machine. Prior to now, she was only able to tolerate five hundred milliliters during a tube feeding. Without her knowledge, I loaded one thousand milliliters into her feeding bag, hoping she could manage it.

She quickly came to accept the plastic feeding tube as a means of life, something that would bring her energy and vitality. Her ignorance of the benefits of the feeding tube washed away, and she came to welcome the fuller life that this extraordinary device had to offer.

The next day, I told her about her one-thousand-milliliter triumph. She remarked that she was upset with herself that she fought the idea of the feeding tube originally. She could not believe how great she felt.

Veronica decided to take her mother shopping for the afternoon. The distance between them had seemed to vanish. Theresa wanted so badly to reconnect with her daughter and perhaps decompress the tension between them over Clark. She made a promise to herself to put that aside and keep her daughter as close to her as she could.

However, when they returned, I could feel an underlying tension coming from her. Veronica only stayed for a short time after that, and a few minutes later, I heard Theresa calling me from her room.

"Everything okay?" I asked.

"Yep. Just really edgy. My mood is so crazy. For no reason, one minute it's great, and the next I'm a wreck."

I asked her about her time with Veronica. They had a great time talking, but she was concerned about Veronica's cavalier mood and her increased isolation from her. "I guess I promised her one life, and now she is forced to live another." She was planning on marrying Clark, which only heightened Theresa's restless state.

Later that evening, I heard talking coming from her bedroom. I stood quietly outside the door. "Just let me go already," she insisted.

She was talking to herself. I knew what she meant. Up to this point, she hadn't taken anything for stress or anxiety. The next morning, we had a long conversation about her state of mind. Behind the scenes, while trying not to die, she was constantly managing everyone's life. Her children were understandable, to a point, but Derek's constant need for reinforcement had added to her already-taxed mind. She insisted she needed him around, but clearly, it was wearing her down.

When Nurse Carly arrived that afternoon, we talked privately before she went up to see Theresa. "I think things are beginning to get to her. Perhaps you could have something prescribed for her." She agreed.

She had mentioned it to Theresa previously, but she was against taking anything that might alter her awareness. But, focusing on controlling any anxiety or depression was important to her overall state of mind.

That afternoon, I filled the prescription for Ativan. Nurse Carly instructed me to give her half the dose, initially. I brought her a glass of water and handed her the pill.

"What's this?"
"Your escape," I told her.

"Annette and I are working through stuff ... She is amazing. I would not be here if it wasn't for her. Not just taking care of me, but almost walking in my shoes ... She picks me up when I fall, pushes me when I am combative (lol ... love that phrase), checks on me but lets me feel I'm still in control. Her humor is amazing... Her no-shit attitude is inspiring. I'm learning to let go of people's problems from my life ... No more letting things drain me."
— From Theresa's Journal

She had fondly named me "Bossy," a title I wore with honor. I didn't just take care of her; I was walking the passage with her. I picked her up when she was down and pushed her when she was a "combative patient." (That was my name for her when she was unwilling to do what was best for her.) Yet, it was important that she still felt in control of her own life.

"I can barely feel my feet," she proclaimed.

I could see the weight lifted from her shoulders. I remembered her plea the night before "to let her go," and in my quest to keep her from giving up, a single pill brought a new sense of calmness that would help her through some of the most challenging times that would lie ahead.

The trust between us was deep. We had many memories as kids growing up that no one else had shared. When I was sixteen, she offered to teach me how to drive a stick shift. She had a 1980 Honda Civic she had managed to buy on her own. We lived on a street that had an adjacent hill that even the best of drivers couldn't conquer using a stick shift. We got off to a tumultuous start. As I pulled away from the curb, I chug, chug, chugged, until the car came to an abrupt halt.

When I think back to those times, it seemed so innocent, but mastering the busy streets and quickly approaching hill seemed almost like a death wish. Yet, my biggest fear wasn't other cars, but rather a stoplight, forcing me to begin the challenge of getting the car moving in a forward motion all over again. As we drove through the flat neighborhood streets, I exultingly could replicate the stop-and-start task repeatedly.

"I think you're ready," she asserted. "Head for the hill!"

Now confident, I wasted no time advancing to the challenge. When we reached the bottom, I felt my head tilt back to view the entire hill.

Perhaps I wasn't quite ready.

"Go!" she charged.

Let's just say I'm glad cell phones weren't around at the time for someone to video record the shameful event. As I reached the beginning of the incline, I paused, holding one foot on the clutch and the other on the gas. We burned rubber the whole way up the hill. Smoke from the tires bellowed past us until we finally reached the crest of the big giant—and came to a neck-jerking halt.

"That was good," she claimed, pushing herself back into her seat. "I'm gonna need new tires, though."

Realizing I could not test myself any further, I pulled the car to the side of the road and let her drive us home. Like now, she put her life in my hands and with the utmost trust; our unwavering bond would never be broken.

In her quest to make sure there would be no issue with the execution of her retirement benefits and life insurance for the kids, I drove her to the Human Resources office at her work.

She wanted to declutter her affairs, so when she was gone, nothing would be left to speculation.

A prestigious hospital in our area called when we were driving home. They had seen her Curriculum Vitae and wanted to offer her the position of chief financial officer. I think she caught him a little off guard when she casually claimed, "I'd love to, but I have terminal cancer."

Over the last several months, she had received several offers for lucrative jobs. This would have been a dream come true a few months back, but now, an unattainable wish.

When we got home, she lay down, and I decided to take Riley for a walk to clear my own head. Matt called me while I was walking and asked how things went. I tried to respond without bursting into tears.

"What's wrong?"

"My day for a meltdown," I claimed. "I'll be home in a bit."

I cried the whole way while walking Riley. I couldn't help but feel defeated. Theresa and I spent so much time together, and at times, I thought I was truly going to save her. When the reality of getting her affairs in order struck me that afternoon, I realized I, too, needed to prepare myself for the nearing end. As I strolled through the park, I avoided anyone who knew me for fear of bellowing into an unmanageable crying jag.

Riley was truly a special soul; he had taught me a great deal about compassion. He could sense my emotions and would fill that space with unconditional love when I was on empty, providing comfort and peace during the most trying times. Strangely enough, he and Theresa seemed to have formed a spiritual bond, bestowing on her a calming effect when she needed it most.

Annette Leeds

Late in the day when I returned from our walk, Theresa was sitting outside at the patio table. "I need to talk to you." Fearing something was wrong and we were heading back to the hospital, I sat down next to her.

"They want me to have chemo."

Confused, I nodded. My first thought was she had received a call from Doctor Reeves.

"Who?" I inquired.

"Derek ... Veronica."

If Theresa's long career in the medical field had taught her nothing else, it was that most terminal patients who elected for aggressive treatment spent their last months suffering from the effects of the therapy. With the strong guidance from Doctor Reeves, she had opted for minimal treatment for her incurable cancer. She chose to spend the balance of her time on earth fighting to be in the moment and feel the best she could under the difficult circumstances.

Even during the initial shock of her diagnosis, she decided very quickly that she didn't want to spend her remaining time strapped to a chair, and then feeling as if she wanted to die just from the consequences of the treatment. She chose not to accept the toxic treatment, contrary to most people when they receive the fatal news.

I realized she was just venting, not necessarily looking for a response. "I had so many things going on in my life. I did what I had to do for my kids to give them a good life. It's tough now sitting here, having to face the reality that I missed so much time with my kids, all the while trying to take care of them."

Sensing something had happened while I was gone, I let her talk. Not long into the conversation, she revealed that

110

she received a telephone call from the oncology department. They were just checking in to see if they could do anything for her or perhaps she had changed her mind about treatment. With pressure from Derek and now the doctor's office, she just needed to voice her anger.

"I guess I only dwell on this on the days when doctors want to count the time I will remain on this earth. I realize they want me to be aware, but some things are better left unsaid. I know I'm dying. I don't need to constantly be reminded of it.

"I am the one dying, yet everyone wants to tell me about their wants and needs ... What about me?" She wiped the corners of her eyes. "I sacrificed me for the good of everyone else. I should have said no or pushed for them to stand on their own two feet."

Gaining her composure, I heard the strength grow in her voice. "Hopefully, I can lead by example. I want my kids to understand that there is a balance. That striving for happiness and success is not out of reach. Christopher will be a success ... Veronica is willing to accept the minimum to get by. That hurts. I want more for her, but she settles for less. These are things I can no longer control. I will be leaving them shortly, and I can only pray they will have learned something from my life."

She loved the sea turtles in Hawaii, and all she wanted to do was return to the trundling flow of the ocean and the turtles swimming gracefully around her. Doctor Reeves had encouraged her several times to take a trip; to do the things she might want to do before she no longer had the strength. Her inability to go in the water seemed to minimize that desire. Reflecting back to all those sunsets she took for granted was perhaps her biggest regret.

Time and time again, she stated she wasn't scared, but rather nervous of what was to come. "I think I have enough angel points," she punned. "So I should be good to go.

"Promise me my funeral won't be boring," she insisted. "But, rather a party for everyone."

She made her wishes abundantly clear, and I was prepared to make a colossal affair when the time came. I knew, in the end, she would die with class, and her funeral would be nothing short of amazing. I refused to write a eulogy, sensing I had many more memories to include. The one thing I knew for sure was it would be a loving eulogy filled with laughter and tears.

Going on a trip would remain a fantasy. I later found out that she truly did want to go to Hawaii, even if it was just to stand on the shoreline and let the water rush over her feet. My mistake was encouraging her to go with Derek or the kids and leave me behind, even if it were just for a few days. Yet, she wouldn't go without me. Our bond together had grown so strong. I realized we would never go back to the little girls "throwing shoes" or who we were without each other, nor would we want to.

While I fought to give her life, she gave my life a jolt. On several occasions, I would try to allow her to have time away from me, either with other family members or her family. Still, the desire to have me by her side was unmistakable. "You'll be right back, right?" she would say. Every memory we made together was new, like having a baby. Each step or special occasion was a first ... but also the last.

She truly looked forward to her appointments with Doctor Reeves. Getting dressed daily was a task at best. Most times, once she completed her grooming rituals, she was so tired all she wanted to do was lie down. Wanting to be fresh for her appointment, she decided to take her shower the night prior.

We had quite a unique ritual for her showers. After covering her drains with waterproof bandages, I would wrap her several times with plastic wrap, followed by waterproof tape to secure the edges.

Standing in the bathroom, she would assume the position while I fortified her abdomen to ensure dryness. Normally, she would cross her arms, cupping both breasts, so I could wrap from her rib cage to her pelvis. Tired from the events of the day, I could only assume she stood daydreaming as I struggled to wrap.

"Okay, are you going to help me?" I inquired. "Or would you prefer I hold your boobs up with my forehead?" We laughed so hard, I nearly wet my pants.

The unusual part of her illness was, as she went through it, things that mattered the most changed, and things you wouldn't think she would look forward to, like a doctor's appointment, became the most rewarding. Her lab tests and CT scans seemed to be holding steady, and, therefore, the month or two she thought would be the end, suddenly seemed to be changing.

This being good news, at the same time, would be surprisingly draining. The time frame was no longer concrete. Was she living a month or a year? Suddenly, making future plans became a task. She vowed to stop worrying about time from that point forward; it felt too much like a game of Russian roulette.

We sat in Doctor Reeves's office, still laughing about the shower incident the night prior. Explaining our giddiness, he laughed. Perhaps not about the story, but the enjoyment he felt seeing her live her life at whatever level that was. He apologized for laughing along, but we were contagious, and she loved that he joined us.

The past year, Theresa's new personification of herself was a single woman wanting to enjoy the company of a man. She wanted so much to have someone she could share her life with, someone that could potentially take care of her. She had grown tired of being the one everyone leaned on, and she hoped she could meet someone that could stand on his own two feet.

Despite the misfortune of her previous relationships, she welcomed the idea of meeting someone new. In recalling the day she first told Margaret and me about Randy, which would also be the first day we would meet him, we were in the car on the way back from the appointment.

"I have a friend stopping by that I haven't seen in a while," she casually stated. "Is six o'clock okay?"

Margaret glanced at me in the back seat as if she had been left out of the loop.

I shrugged. "Yeah. Whatever works."

Margaret responded, "We'll make ourselves scarce."

We teased her as if we were in junior high.

"We are just friends," she proclaimed. As she described him as the "love of her life," "friends" wasn't the first word that popped into my head.

"He's married," she insisted. "But, we are just friends."

Theresa was truly a traditionalist, an old-fashioned girl, despite her forward exterior. She was used to working in a man's world; she worked hard to get to the top, so her persona was assertive and resolute. Yet, inside, all she wanted was someone to spend her time with, someone that could make her laugh, and at the same time, maybe someone with traits comparable to her own.

She had met Randy at the hospital where she worked. They had a strong bond, and that was all. They flirted and laughed. He gave her hope to believe that there were men out there that seemed to have it all. He was confident and bold, which was a refreshing quality she craved to find in a man.

When we got back to Margaret's house, she changed her outfit into a sporty summer dress with sandals and jewelry to match. Randy hadn't seen her since she became ill. She was worried that the shock of her thin appearance might make him feel uneasy. She wanted to feel in control and confident, not a patient looking for sympathy in her last dying days.

Known for being the "neighborhood watch," Margaret would stand at her kitchen window, making sure no strange doings were happening in her neighborhood. Theresa and I called her "Mrs. Kravitz" from the television show *Bewitched*. We used to make fun of her while she snapped photos of her neighbors she suspected of doing suspicious deeds.

She repeatedly told her husband about the neighborhood oddities, but he never seemed convinced or affected by her crazy antics. He was more concerned about someone getting angry or filing a complaint if someone caught her.

That afternoon, she stood steady at her post, waiting for Randy to show up. Margaret ordered me to get my things together so we could leave the house on a moment's notice when he arrived.

Theresa smirked at me, shaking her head. "You guys don't need to leave," Theresa said nervously.

Hank asserted, "Can I just stay in the back room?"

"Just stay," she insisted. "You don't need to hide in the back room. Margaret's nuts."

Ignoring her plea, Margaret rushed from her post through the kitchen. "He's here, he's here!"

I was in stitches as she ran back and forth, calling for Theresa. On her last lap around the kitchen, her purse strap caught on the junk drawer, yanking her backward and almost to the ground.

Theresa waved her arm at us, trying not to laugh as she went to answer the door. Worried her eldest sister would surely cause a scene, she scolded her silently to gain her composure. I held my side and stretched my face hoping to stop the cramps brought on by laughing so hard.

Theresa answered the door as if everything were normal, ignoring the commotion going on behind the scenes. In walked a tall man, barely able to clear the doorjamb. He was wearing jeans and a white Polo shirt. His short torso and long legs gave the appearance that his belt was strapped just underneath his chest.

Exhilarated by his visit, Theresa grabbed his hand and escorted him into the kitchen to meet us. Clearly thrilled by their relationship, but she also understood it had its limitations; she could remain close to him and confide in him, but the relationship would never be intimate. She remained true to her old-school views. He was married, and she would never do anything that might jeopardize that. However, she adored him and what his modest, intelligent wit represented.

Looking back on the months that followed, she enjoyed the brief times she would have with him. Mostly, late-evening telephone calls, where I would hear a contagious giggle coming from her room. I think she was happy with the fact she had someone willing to sit and talk about whatever events of the day, with no mention of her impending condition. He was very spiritual as well, and I think that provided peace for her. His mother had passed less than a year prior, and Theresa said the wounds for him were still deep. Perhaps he avoided her condition because he did not want to face the sorrow of losing someone else close to him in such a short time.

Theresa always seemed to be running toward something that was just out of reach. She may not have caught everything she was chasing, but she enjoyed life and the challenges that it brought. I don't think she realized the lives she impacted; she had touched so many people, and I sensed that when she was gone, her memories would induce much endless laughter as well as limitless tears.

Meanwhile, Phyllis was growing increasingly aware that her job as the executor of Theresa's estate was looming. Perhaps Theresa chose her to handle her children's affairs specifically because of Phyllis's unwavering character. Strong-willed and always looking at the causes and not just the effects of a situation; never allowing emotion to stop her. At times, Theresa expressed apprehension that she might be too strict, but realized it was the best choice for the task that lay ahead for her children.

Phyllis, I guess being the fourth child, would be considered in the middle of the pack. Growing up, she went through an array of personality traits. In her twenties, she was somewhat of a wild child, searching for what might suit her life going forward. However, as she settled into her adult life, she seemed to shift toward a resentful grown-up. As difficult as it was to watch, I think this was, ultimately, what drove her to be the person she longed to become. As she got older, either by necessity or by design, she seemed to find her own identity, becoming more and more independent, furthering her career. I think once she began to direct her energies elsewhere, she finally settled into what she wanted in life. Being a very private person, she kept her feelings to herself most times. But, it was clear that she held herself to a higher standard and expected nothing less from those around her.

Theresa looked forward to her evenings spent with Phyllis, yet, at times, grew drained of the conversations of what to do when she was gone. "I don't want to talk about this anymore," she stated. "I did my best, and whatever it is, it is." She wanted to talk about her future, even though she had nothing planned.

She began reading again. Mostly trashy novels, but on occasion, she would grab a book on making sense of death, while still trying to live life. Those books, however, were limited. Not many people seemed to have the same outlook she did about continuing her life. She pushed herself forward, seeing death as an imposing unsettled visitor, knowing it was there waiting for her, yet, still making the best of the life she had remaining.

"I know I'm dying, but what am I doing until that time?" she demanded. "I should be living."

She refused to live her life stagnantly. She realized thinking about the future only dragged her down. Living in the moment from sunup to sundown seemed to be the most rewarding. Trying to imagine her life on any trajectory other than what was right in front of her made her depressed. Therefore, she chose to live each moment with the utmost respect. She had given herself a fantastic life and wasn't going to waste a single minute wallowing in the "what-ifs?"

Over the next few weeks, her strength seemed to diminish. Derek's job laid him off, and now, he looked to Theresa to handle his affairs, once again. I still wasn't sure if she was just ignorant of his games, or she resolved herself to the fact that he was her Achilles' heel. Either way, I just wanted to wring this guy's neck.

One late afternoon she received a telephone call from him. He seemed to be at a loss for words and was having trouble understanding an e-mail he received regarding a job offer.

She didn't quite understand his confusion. The e-mail seemed straightforward. Having a history of high blood pressure and being a smoker, she feared he was having a stroke. Without hesitation, she told him to have someone drive him to the emergency room. He was admitted for testing, and she waited nervously for the outcome.

Later that evening, she told me Veronica was going to take her to the hospital in the morning to see him. I was concerned, and I expressed my feelings, but the choice was hers. She had been fatigued as of late and didn't seem to bounce back as easily as she did a few months back.

The next morning, she told me she wasn't going to go see Derek. "I just don't think it's good for me right now. I'll wait and see what they decide for his care. At least for today."

Yet, that night she changed her mind once again. "I need to be there for him," she claimed. "Margaret is going to come get me."

I didn't react to the news. She knew I was annoyed with her, mostly because she had worked so hard to keep healthy, yet now, she's willing to place herself at risk when his family was there to keep her up to date. The visit with him was short, but she was glad she went. He suffered a mild stroke that he would manage with medication.

"I had to yell at him," she said. "He promised he would be there for my children."

In my mind, I was thinking, *Yeah, right. He doesn't even have the sense to take care of himself.*

I truly believed he was in a contest with her to see if he could kill himself first before she died. With all his health issues, I caught him on numerous occasions smoking, which he assured her he had stopped. He knew I had seen him, and I was sure he wondered why I kept it to myself. Because not only was it not my business, I didn't want Theresa to have to worry about anything else. While she was at the hospital with him, he confessed to her about his smoking, thinking I must have ratted him out. She later asked me why I didn't say anything.

"Not my place to say anything," I told her. "He wants to kill himself, so go for it."

I had my own issues to deal with, and I certainly wasn't about to take on the problems of someone with whom I had no connection. Over time, he would grow increasingly bothered by me. Honestly, I didn't care. She was *my* sister, *my* house, *my* rules. I witnessed, firsthand, him putting her through stress and turmoil. I realized how she had come to this point in her life, people constantly draining the life out of her, until she had no more to give. My job was to protect her and keep her from harm, and if that meant making a few enemies along the way, then so be it.

Chapter 11

Mom and Dad stopped by for a visit, which was usually every day, unless we were at the hospital or a doctor's appointment. Dad appeared to be getting more and more forgetful, and Mom feared he had early stages of Alzheimer's, something that ran in his family. As the illness seemed to be progressing, so were his mood swings. Most times, it was a mystery as to what would set off the tantrum, but he seemed increasingly ornery, especially toward Mom.

"I need a new wife," he'd say. "I'm getting rid of her."

Usually, the change stemmed from a control issue. He didn't want anyone giving him instructions. She commented that his driving seemed to be more of a challenge as of late.

"He scares me," she said. "He stopped the other day so far back from the intersection. I asked him why, and he had no answer."

He seemed like he was trying to get back to a time when he had full control of his family. Here was this powerful person, disappearing before our eyes. Theresa's condition, I think, was the stimulus to his deteriorating condition, taxing his mental strength.

Comprehending what lay ahead was far too difficult for him to face, and trying to cope with the multitude of feelings he was experiencing on top of it proved to be too much. Perhaps he was withdrawing, in search of some way to ask for mercy. I don't believe he had the wherewithal to handle his dying daughter.

He had drastically diminished his weekly church visits. Clearly, his cognitive functions had changed in the last few months, and he was very unstable on his feet at times. Although, I don't believe that was the root of his "absence," rather, I can only imagine he felt his faith was betraying him by stealing one of his children.

One morning, I decided I probably should start getting back to an exercise regimen. Most days just seemed to run into one another for me. Taking care of Theresa's needs consumed most of my day, and I was tired. However, I needed to make some time for myself in between everything. I had been eating a lot of fast food and having an occasional drink when I was at Margaret's house, habits I usually avoided up until the last few months.

I jumped on the treadmill in the garage and managed to get through about fifteen harsh minutes of walking, before needing to stop to catch my breath—a far cry from the thirty-minute runs I did without hesitation the previous summer.

I began to look forward to these sessions. It not only helped increase my energy level, it became a huge stress reliever as well. Some days, I was an angry jogger, and other days, I was an emotional jogger. With my headphones blaring, it gave me an escape, allowing my mind to run free, and it made me feel good.

In the early morning hours, while jogging, I glanced down at my phone and realized Theresa had sent me a text message.

I did something really bad. Where are you?

I jumped off the treadmill and rushed up the stairs.

She stood staring in the bathroom mirror, holding a newly cut feeding hose in one hand, while trying to keep the other end from slipping into her belly. I glanced down at the counter and saw a pair of scissors. "What happened?"

She was clearly shocked by what had just transpired and a little shaky. "I tried to help; I was doing the dressing change. But, when I went to cut the tape next to the tube, I cut straight through the hose."

She tried to own her blunder, which made it that much more entertaining. She could only describe her misstep in putting a hairclip on in the mirror.

"It looked one way, but clearly it was another."

"It'll be okay." I couldn't help but chuckle at her comparison. "Just don't let the other end fall out."

I quickly taped it down to her skin, providing some stability so she didn't have to stand there and hold it. She realized I wasn't panicking, and, therefore, she didn't panic.

I called Nurse Carly, who told me to go to the local hospital instead of having to drive all the way out to see Doctor Reeves. I agreed and hoped Theresa would be open to the plan. We had talked about possibly going to the closer facility in case of an emergency, but I didn't realize we would be doing it so soon. I quickly changed my sweaty clothes, and we hurried to the emergency room.

All I can say is hospital emergency rooms need to train their staff to adapt to terminally ill patients. When we arrived, the waiting room was relatively empty; yet, we had to wait an excessive amount of time. I calmly explained to the triage nurse her condition, but she seemed uninterested and continued with her daily tasks. Theresa's pain was spiking; exhaustion was taking over and she needed to lie down. I asked the nurse for a mask for her; the last thing I needed was her catching something while waiting to get help. She gave me a blank stare like this was an obscene request.

"A *mask*," I repeated. "Do you have a mask I can give her?"

All those clichés about emergency rooms were true. "You realize her feeding tube needs to be changed within an allotted time, right?"

Sarcastically, she responded, "We don't normally do this in the emergency room."

I completely came unglued. "Can you tell by her face she is in no shape to be sitting here for *four hours*? Yet, *now*, you are telling me you are not sure who handles this?" Finally, after much bantering, she paged the general surgeon on call.

Not long after, a young doctor with gray-peppered hair arrived. He introduced himself as Doctor Miles, apologized for the confusion, and explained they were feverishly looking for the proper feeding tube. He introduced us to Doctor Jeffries, the general surgery resident shadowing him for the day.

We were no stranger to medical residents following Doctor Reeves, but this resident was pompous and dismissive. He was average height, but with remarkably small feet. So much so, you couldn't help but notice. Even throughout her pain and discomfort, Theresa managed to shoot me a look toward the floor at his feet.

The doctor conversed with Theresa, apologetically, and assured her they would solve the feeding tube issue shortly. He had the nurse start an IV line for hydration and prescribed some pain and nausea medication to keep her at ease. He ordered blood tests while she rested comfortably.

Residents customarily make medical judgments without the input of the attending, but Jeffries seemed to be taking his job just a little too far. "I don't think we are going to be able to replace the tube. Your liver enzymes are too high."

Theresa was on edge; she wasn't at her normal hospital, and these two were not Doctor Reeves. She snapped at him. "I have pancreatic cancer. Of course, my enzymes are high."

His inexperience suddenly turned to anger as Theresa insisted he got Doctor Miles. I could see in his eyes that he considered her pointless, already obsolete rather than a patient. He just wanted to mark her off his list and move on to something else.

After six painstaking hours, the feeding tube was finally in place. Doctor Miles checked on her one last time and signed her release. In all the confusion, he realized the cap for the feeding tube was missing.

"I don't have a spare plug," he remarked. Without hesitation, he grabbed the cap to a ballpoint pen and jammed it over the opening. "That should work."

By his response, I could only imagine the shocked look on my face. I realized I had better get my sister the hell out of there before something else happened. If cancer didn't kill her, one of these two fools might pull it off.

Rain or shine, the epic traffic we endured, taking the fifty-five-mile freeway journey to the hospital to see Doctor Reeves always turned into a two-hour car-jammed commute. However, despite it all, the good he did for Theresa far outweighed the bad on any given day, which was why we chose to make the long drives to see Doctor Reeves. It was important that she had a doctor she was able to talk to, be comfortable with, a doctor she knew would see to it that she received excellent care, and a doctor who would give it to her straight, with no chaser, but with a lot of compassion. When we arrived home, I realize he didn't stitch the new tube to her skin, so it was threatening to slide out. I anchored it with some butterfly tape to secure it against her skin.

That evening, her pain climbed higher and higher. I couldn't seem to get her comfortable no matter what I did. Such a small incident was proving to be a catastrophic event. I checked her dressings and flushed her biliary drain. With each force of the saline through the syringe, bile leaked from around her feeding tube.

It was late, but I knew I needed to take her to see Doctor Reeves. I packed her bag as she rolled back and forth on the bed in distress. I was concerned now that the doctor at the emergency room may have perforated something when he inserted the feeding tube. The long drive to Doctor Reeves would surely prove faster than heading back to that horrendous emergency room in the hopes of getting a doctor that knew what he was doing.

It was 3:00 a.m. when we arrived at Margaret's house. Thankfully, Theresa slept most of the drive. We decided to rest there for a few hours until we could reach someone at Doctor Reeves's office.

Our hero to the rescue once again . . . Shortly after eight, we arrived at his office to see him.

He glanced at the pen cap covering the opening and shook his head.

"Don't ask," Theresa said.

He apologized for the other hospital and continued repairing the work done by the incompetence the day before. He ordered a CT scan and arranged for interventional radiology to check the biliary drain, which hadn't had any output since yesterday.

Once in radiology, they decided to inject the CT scan contrast, Gastrografin, into her feeding tube, rather than make her drink it. She appreciated their recommendation, being nauseous and in so much pain already. Drinking what she described as "nuclear waste" would have proved disastrous.

Once back at Margaret's house, she was finally able to get some sleep. Margaret worked early the following morning, so Theresa and I went to see Doctor Reeves alone for the CT scan results. I was exhausted, yet a thunderous sound in the house jarred me awake. I glanced at my phone. It was only 5:00 a.m. I thought perhaps I was dreaming, but as I sat on the edge of the bed, I heard the bathtub running.

I got up and glanced into the bedroom where Theresa slept. She was not there. I heard feverish sloshing in the bathroom. I knocked and entered the bathroom without waiting for a response. She was kneeling next to the tub, rinsing the bedsheets.

"Theresa?"

She was crying, and panic covered her face. "What's the matter?"

Struggling to catch her breath, she said, "I crapped all over the bed. I didn't even know it. I just woke up. It was wet; it's *everywhere*." She was clearly weak, but her adrenaline kept her in motion.

I grabbed her under both arms and lifted her up. "I got it," I claimed.

She stood naked in the bathroom, crying. I felt so horrible for her. She was such a proud person, and this brought on a wave of shame. I grabbed a robe and put it around her.

Scooping up the sheets, I tossed them in the washing machine and quickly attended to her. "Come on, let's get you cleaned up."

Quickly, the incident was behind us. Usually prone to constipation, the rush of diarrhea caught her off guard. She feared something was terribly wrong and was concerned about what the CT scan would show.

I didn't say much to her about her condition unless she brought it up or if something required medical attention. Maybe there was something wrong with me, but I chose to avoid the obvious and waited for the surprise ending. Morbid, I know, but I think that is what kept my sanity. In the beginning, I used to count the days, knowing they only gave her three to six months to live. I told myself to stop; I finally let go of the notion that I could control what was happening to her—or me—at that point. I needed to just go with the flow; take the punches as they came. When I finally came to that realization, it was freeing, I winged it from that point forward, and it sure made life a little less stressful.

Each day, Theresa took the time to reflect on all the good times, embrace her agonizing failures, and cherish our time together, filling each day with vivacity and love. She replaced fear with faith; she treasured the time she had and lived it with no regrets. She chose to sidestep conversations with those who only wanted to talk about her cancer. "Talk to me about clothes or something else," she insisted. "But, staring at me like I'm already one foot in the grave makes me want to stay away from everyone."

"Cancer . . . How did I get here? Why me? Why now? All things I ask myself, but it really doesn't matter. It's here, and I have to deal with it. I hate what this thing is doing to my body. Being thin was a dream for me, but not as a dying woman. It is perhaps the hardest thing for me to accept. I don't feel attractive with these drains . . . They save my life, so I deal with it. I still feel pretty positive about my future . . . Yet, I worry every time I look in the mirror . . . My face is pale, and my spirit doesn't seem as strong. I'm working on that. I need to keep my edge."

— From Theresa's Journal

Lying on the exam table in Doctor Reeves's office, she closed her eyes. The room was quiet, and she told me how much she appreciated everything. I told her not to worry; everything would be okay. Yet, I sensed she thought the words were hollow wishes.

When Doctor Reeves entered the room, her eyes lit up; his confidence filled the room, giving her power to keep going. As the CT scan illuminated on the computer screen, he sat close to her, reviewing the images.

"Everything looks good," he claimed. "How are you feeling?"

He helped her sit up.

"Are you sure? I had something really bad happen last night, and I thought there must be a serious problem. Nothing has changed?"

"Nope, it looks good. What happened?" He glanced over at me as she began to talk.

She was clearly embarrassed to tell him about her voracious diarrhea that had overcome her early that morning.

"It was horrible. The worst part is I never even woke up until it was all over."

The day prior, at his request, they injected the CT scan concoction into her feeding tube. Without hesitation, he apologized, explaining that is a side effect from the imaging contrast. "No one told you?" Apologizing again, he assured her the scan looked good, and she shouldn't be embarrassed.

She grabbed his hand and thanked him, perhaps for giving her the courage to feel right about herself once again. She tried hard not to allow herself to get sidetracked by her fate. Sometimes, though, it knocked her down. Most times, it was when she felt like her identity was being compromised. She was determined to push herself to feel normal, but that wasn't always easy.

That night, she visited me in my dreams. At first, I only saw a tree-lined dirt path, and then finally from behind the trees, she poked her head out and then headed away from me. I called her name several times, but she didn't seem to hear me. Finally, casually, she turned back toward me, smiled, waved, and then turned back around, strolling down the path. Suddenly, I was awakened by the sound of her voice. I jumped out of bed and stood quietly for a moment to see if she was calling me out of my sleep. The house was still, only the sound of a cricket that had gotten into the house.

I walked down the hallway. Her room had never seemed so quiet. As I entered, all I could see was her still body lying in bed. I got close to her to check her breathing. It was shallow but peaceful. Sensing my presence staring over her, she awoke. "You okay?" she inquired.

She had such a rough time the night before after soiling the bed, I think she thought I was concerned about a repeat performance. She did a snow angel with her arms across the bed. "It's not wet."

"I know, I just thought I heard you call me."

She had been showing all the signs they tell you that comes when death is imminent. A burst of energy followed by withdrawal from loved ones, and then lots of sleeping. She did that all week, and my mind had me fearing the end was near.

I didn't say much to many people about her condition. I was afraid I wouldn't be able to hold it together if someone asked me how she was. Most times, when you reveal something so devastating to people, all you get is a catchy phrase to try to make you feel better. Stupid, I know, but I learned this lesson the hard way. When one of the checkers at the grocery store asked me how she was doing, and I completely fell apart in the checkout lane. I guess this was my version of self-preservation. I just hoped I could handle the end.

Phyllis came over, and Theresa told her about her humiliating bed-crapping incident. By now, she had found the comedy in it. As she tried to explain the systematic shock she was in and the crippling panic, she couldn't catch her breath from laughing so hard. Phyllis didn't want to disrespect the mortification she must have felt, but Theresa had clearly seen the humor in it.

"This wasn't a sneak-a-fart-out-and-no-one-will-notice kind of thing," she claimed. "This was a holy-crap-I-shit-the-bed terror."

Contrary to the last few weeks, she was perky and ready for adventure. She wanted to look good for Camille's upcoming wedding, so we decided to venture into the backyard to bathe in the sun, as it poured out its brilliant hot oranges and reds down on us. That same sun, with all its beautiful, warm rays, gave Theresa a pretty nice tan, while I was still pasty white. My beauty rituals had flown out the window of late. I needed to get back on track before everyone started thinking *I* was the patient. However, for that little time spent in the backyard, life felt almost normal.

We talked about the feeding tube schedule; she must spend up to twelve hours on the continuous feeding to get in the proper amount of nutrition. Although she didn't have a deep love for the feeding process, she embraced its necessity. Watching people around her eat and enjoy the things they loved was difficult. But, throwing up anything the minute it hit her stomach was even worse for her. Even though she only consumed water and clear broth at this point, oftentimes, that didn't even stay down. We had to split her continuous feeding schedule, and even that was becoming taxing.

Christopher called his mom to talk about his school schedule for the fall. He wanted to take some classes that didn't coincide with his major. Theresa was trying to keep him focused on college, but at times, it fell on deaf ears. She told Christopher he needed to start thinking of the future and what lay ahead. She was trying to teach him to think things through before making rushed decisions.

"When I'm dead, you won't have me to bounce things off of, so you need to start making better choices," she calmly said.

"What is there to say other than I couldn't be more proud of you. You jumped in with both feet; it was hard, but it was your fresh start. You're doing it . . . Remember, at the end of the day, if you just half ass through because being the party guy is fun, everyone else will have the awesome degree and job . . . and you'll still be holding the party hat. Time to learn balance . . . If you manage your time, it all works."

— From Theresa's Journal

Her comment seemed harsh, but necessary. She was trying to get her twenty-year-old son to turn into a man quicker than his hormones would allow. Theresa had a corkboard in the corner of her room. There, she posted positive thoughts and notes she wrote to remind herself of all the things she wanted to accomplish for her children. She filled that board day after day with endless notes and reminders. One of the notes was particularly profound. I'm not sure whom she meant the note for—her or them.

"Follow your intuition. Never second-guess those little hairs that warn you when they stand up on the back of your neck." — From Theresa's Journal

Chapter 12

Her first meeting with her palliative doctor was at my home, and a far cry from the oncologist she met at the hospital. Doctor Jindal was a slender man with thinning hair and dim, green eyes. Seeing death firsthand is foreign to most of us, but he was all too familiar with its presence. Knowing it by a look, smell, or sound must be a skill none of us would welcome. Yet, his spirit was refreshing, and his casual demeanor made me feel he was here not only for her but for all of us as well.

"I was really worried about our meeting," she confessed.

"Why's that?"

"Well, the oncologist that referred me to your staff was very grim. I guess I just wasn't up for it today."

She told him she was fighting with all her might to stay here, if God would allow it. "There is always someone that wants to remind me that time is passing, but I don't listen," she claimed. "I got it; trust me, I'm the one living it. I don't need to be constantly reminded. I'm pleasantly surprised each morning when I awake and try to make the best of each day."

He sat on the chair next to her bed, rubbing the top of Riley's head as he spoke. "Well, I don't work that way." He welcomed Riley, her protector, something that meant more to her than anything. "Is he your dog?"

"No, my sister's. But, he gets me. He's my soul mate. He knows just how to make me feel better when my day goes sideways."

"Well, you're lucky to have him, and he you." He smiled.

As she sat on the edge of the bed, she began to shake like a tree in the wind. He reached over and felt her forehead.

"You cold?" he inquired.

"No, I just feel really weak."

Riddled with hot flashes over the last week, she was concerned about their meaning. He told her based on her last lab tests, her cancer markers were up, but he believed the hot flashes were due to an underlying infection. It was like a thrust in the stomach for her when he gave her the news. The constant infections seemed to become the norm. It was not if, but when another would occur. When these bouts of infection would knock her down, the days seemed shorter. The medication took a toll on her, causing her to sleep more, taking away precious time, taxing her state of being. It was very depressing for her when she couldn't control certain things.

He asked about the severity of her pain and nausea, something she could no longer hide. She told him the bad days were getting more frequent and, despite the endless feedings, she continued to drop weight, which caused her the most anxiety.

He gave her great comfort, advocating for her to live the life she wanted. I'll never forget the words he told her as he left that day. He told her to aim for a different kind of target. "We cannot stop this voyage you are on, but maybe we can make the seas a little less turbulent."

He encouraged her to embrace the medications rather than fight them, giving her the spirit to continue rather than allowing the pain to knock her down. As he left, he told her to follow-up with Doctor Reeves. He was concerned about the possibility of infection and thought she needed to make a trip to see him.

The biliary drain had clogged, once again. As Doctor Reeves tried to force 10 ccs of saline through the hose, the excruciating pain caused her to recoil as the solution sprayed back. He told her that she should be able to tolerate 100 ccs without any problem. It was clear she had another infection stemming from her feeding tube, surrounding granulation tissue, which is a common complication as the body tries to heal what it thinks is a wound. He cauterized the pinkish tissue with silver nitrate. She winced as he laid the stick over the affected area.

"You okay?" he asked.

She nodded for him to continue.

Her constant battle with constipation was now also becoming a topic of concern. He told her that without getting that under control, a bowel obstruction would be imminent. He was not trying to scare her, but knowing surgery would not be an option at this point, he was zealous about avoiding that situation.

Early Saturday morning, I packed the car to leave Margaret's house. She and Theresa talked at the kitchen table; yet, with each pass I made, her face became paler and more fraught.

"What's the matter?"

She burst into tears, which didn't happen often. "It isn't working. The drain stopped working. Eventually, it is going to stop altogether, and that will be it."

I responded like a superhero. "I know, but that isn't today."

We called interventional radiology, and they squeezed her in for another drain change. It was a weekend, so we needed to go through the emergency room for the appointment.

Margaret dropped us off at the entrance and went to find a parking spot. When she got inside, they were checking us in at the desk. A tall, slightly overweight male nurse was speaking to her quietly over the counter. He motioned for her to come behind the half door where he sat.

"I need to tell you something," he said, as he gently put his arm around her.

"Me?" she said.

He quietly escorted her back to a bed ahead of the other people. I knew what he was doing. With all our endless trips to the hospital, we had seen him on many occasions, and he must have sensed her despair. Turns out his uncle had just been diagnosed with pancreatic cancer. Maybe it was a pay-it-forward moment, but in any event, she truly appreciated it.

We still had to wait several hours for Doctor Kim to get to her; he had a few procedures in front of her. At least she was comfortable in a bed and getting some pain relief. Jasmine was her nurse for the time being. She was so gentle with her. Most of the nurses were wonderful, but when you are there as much as we were, you would see some bad ones, too. You wonder why they ever went into the medical field, to begin with.

The doctor performed a balloon procedure around the tube to eliminate the sludge that was continually forming and clogging the drain. Yes, "sludge" is a medical term. I had heard this term used freely by the doctors, so I looked it up. There it was "sludge," a mixture of cholesterol from the body mixing with the bile, which formed a slow-moving slush.

She claimed the pain was better, and her sides were extremely sore. "I feel like I've been in a boxing match."

Understandably so, they had been in and out of her liver with this drain three times in the last two weeks. The hose was stiff and unforgiving, wearing against her skin. They sedated her during the procedure, so she was quite groggy when she returned. She hadn't had her feedings in two nights, so I asked the emergency doctor if they could give her some IV fluids to rehydrate and recharge her.

Margaret and I decided to go to the cafeteria for something to eat. We had been at the hospital most of the day and hadn't eaten anything, which was a common occurrence on our trauma excursion. Margaret kept a stream of treats in her car, mostly healthy snacks, which I always double-downed on with some junk food. My waistline was clearly reflecting my new diet regimen; my yoga pants had now become my new best friend.

We were supposed to have Mother's Day at my house tomorrow. I texted everyone and canceled. I called Mom to tell her what was happening. I'm sure her heart dropped to her feet. She wanted so badly to be there for her daughter, but she didn't have the strength. She was battling two war fronts— Dad's declining mental state and trying to be there for her daughter.

Dad was having his own issues, so he spent most of his time in bed sleeping, leaving her alone to ponder the looming outcome. His dementia seemed to be worsening with each day he had to face Theresa's fate. For once in his life, he didn't seem to have the answers. Struggling over the thought of losing his daughter caused him mental anguish. His processor was failing, and his internal fight was like being in a bed of sea kelp, entangled and pulling him down with each rush of disappointment.

In typical Mom style, she said, "What do I do with all the food?"

I told her that was not the concern at this point. She realized how silly it sounded and retracted her statement.

Later that evening, Theresa called Veronica. She wanted to make sure someone was picking Christopher up from the airport, but she got no answer. The endless calls seemed like they would never stop. Finally, in the early morning, Veronica responded, claiming she was in the shower.

"You've been in the shower for three days?" Theresa ranted. "I've been calling you, and you don't answer me."

I told Theresa not to worry and arranged for a car service to get him from the airport.

"She kills me," Theresa said.

"I got it covered; don't frustrate yourself with this. He'll be home soon."

"Do you feel up to driving back?" I asked. "We can go back home now and still get everyone together for Mother's Day."

"Yeah, let's go," she insisted. "I'll be fine."

I rallied the family for Mother's Day even though I was not in the mood. I dreaded these get-togethers because while I enjoyed spending time with everyone, there were always a few I could have written off as wasted space.

After she hadn't seen or spoken to Theresa in a while, our niece, Malory, graced us with her presence. She spent quite a bit of time with Theresa before she got sick, primarily because she was trying to get into the fire department and needed help with applications and résumés. We weren't strangers to Malory's selfishness, and her lack of regard for others was undeniable. I had grown tired of it; we had a standing joke between us about her. "Okay, back to me."

That afternoon proved no different. When I questioned her about her absence, she insisted, "It is just too difficult on me to see her like this. It really bothers me."

My eyebrows arched at her response. How much more self-centered could she be? I wanted to say, "How do you think she feels? She's the one dying," but the response wasn't worth the energy it would take.

It finally became painfully clear why Malory had come that day. She needed Theresa to tweak an admissions letter for her. It still amazed me how people's priorities can get so screwed up, and then act devastated when things happen around them.

I felt oddly restless that day, in a strange sort of way. People were always worried about how a situation would affect them, not taking into consideration the one who was suffering. This was so textbook Malory. I paced around the house, feeling an inner tension. I wanted to throw her out, but knew it would surely cause unneeded friction, so I chose to keep my mouth shut.

Later that evening, I lay at the foot of Theresa's bed, and we talked. By all outward appearances, Theresa looked great the last few weeks. However, she told me, she felt different.

"What do you mean?"

"I just don't bounce back like I used to. Things are progressing, and I feel it. I keep telling my kids I am running out of time, but they don't seem to get it."

Times like this I realized how in tune she was with her inner self. Collectively, everyone saw things differently and from different perspectives and how her passing would affect them. I noticed this, especially in Veronica. She seemed self-absorbed on the surface, but I think she truly was scared to lose her mother and therefore, avoided precious time with her. I fear she'd wind up in therapy at forty years old when she realizes she should have capitalized on these valuable moments.

Theresa's disappointment was visible. She wanted to spend time with her daughter, which was a personal loss she could not hide. She worried now more about Christopher, fearing his sister would not be there for him either. I assured her he would not be alone.

She tried to refrain from being protective of her daughter, but rather, tried to empower her. I felt like she was methodically trying to take parts of herself and give them to her daughter for strength. She knew Christopher would need to lean on Veronica when she was gone and wanted to develop that fierce instinct in her eldest child.

"It's okay to be frustrated with me; remember, that's my job. I believe you are stronger than all of us combined, and the day you realize that, you will begin to kick butt like you were meant to. Remember, tough love is better than letting someone just skate by. You have a voice; use it . . . People who truly love you will respect you, and in the end, you will be happier. Take control, but with respect. Don't be the mom, be the leader. I will always be there holding your hand."

— From Theresa's Journal

On her most emotional days, I used humor to distract her. As a widening array of memories filled the void of her daughter's presence, they never matched up to the time they spent together.

Her changing perspective on life invigorated Theresa. Having battled through such difficult times, she realized that even her worst upsets had helped her harvest some of the most important lessons. Dealing with those challenges had left her eternally changed. This situation would be no different.

She tried to accept her daughter's actions, but didn't like it. Even in the darkest moments, she kept faith that they would change, so she forced herself to push forward. "Life goes on," she insisted. Her proclamation was unquestionable; she knew she didn't have the time to change anyone else's course.

She decided she would begin taking the sleeping pills prescribed. She had fought the idea in the past; I think she feared she wouldn't wake up. Lying awake at night, worrying, was becoming draining; she became keenly aware that sleep was an important part of her health.

That night, I grabbed the sleeping pill from her medicine cabinet. She put her hand out like a spoiled child, and in one motion, threw it to the back of her throat, and swallowed. She gulped down a mouthful of water and lay back down. No resistance; the barriers were coming down.

The house was quiet; Matt and Riley were in bed. I was exhausted, but I just didn't want to be idle. I began cleaning up downstairs. I thought about what Doctor Reeves had told us from the beginning. He said, "We call it dwindling." I didn't truly understand what he meant at the time, but as time was passing, it made perfect sense. Her cancer wasn't like falling off a sharp cliff, but rather slowly and systematically, her body would deceive her.

Feeling exhilarated, we headed to Camille's wedding in San Diego. The affair was to run the entire weekend. Sophie, Theresa, and I traveled together. We piled the car high with bags and medical devices for our weekend getaway. Traveling with Sophie was always a bit of a challenge because she seemed to bring everything she owned. Accompanied by all the gear we needed for Theresa, the car was quite cozy.

We arrived early at the hotel and decided to go to the mall to kill some time before everyone else arrived. The shopping area consisted of high-end boutique stores and one exclusive department store. Sophie needed to use the restroom, so I pushed Theresa in the wheelchair to the women's clothes. Adjacent to us was the shoe department. After some time passed, I heard Sophie talking to a salesperson. The refined gentleman stood rigid as he caught a whiff of the air-biscuit Sophie quietly released.

"What's that smell?" Theresa asked. "Is that sissy torturing the help? I guess she never made it to the bathroom."

I rapidly pushed her through the rack of clothes slapping across her face, like going through the brushes at a car wash, trying to get away from the noxious odor.

"Hang on, the hangers are caught on the wheelchair," she yelped.

We watched from afar as the salesman, desperate to make a sale, stood his ground, awaiting her request. Looking back at us, Sophie shrugged and smiled.

"We'll stay over here," I announced. "Let us know when the fog clears."

The night before the big day, we visited with family and friends and then turned in early for some girl time. I brought

my do-it-yourself facial kit, slathering the girls with their green masks. Sophie and I shared a queen bed and let Theresa have her own.

Later that night, Theresa and I were awakened by what seemed like a wild animal in the room. I took my phone out and recorded the ravenous noises coming from Sophie's body.

"Is that her snoring?" Theresa asked.

"Yep. I think she might suck me in." I giggled.

By this point, we were laughing so hard I could barely hold the phone still.

"I'm not going to get any sleep," she claimed. "Throw a pillow over her head."

Sophie awoke, delirious. "Am I snoring?"

"Uh, yeah," I responded, holding my phone up, replaying the audio over and over.

This was all too reminiscent of our childhood. Every sibling seemed to have his or her quirk. Our sister, Phyllis, was an avid sleepwalker. Many a night, Theresa and I would belly crawl to Phyllis's room to watch the show. Some nights were quiet with no action, but other nights were pure entertainment. We started bringing our pillows with us on the journey in case we needed to cover our faces. Oftentimes, her behavior brought such hilarity we almost woke the whole house with our thunderous snickering.

We spent the next morning getting ready and snapping photos with each other, and then boarded the shuttle to go to the venue. Several people at the wedding knew Theresa, and I think her stunning exterior shocked them. Her coping mechanism was amazing; she always knew how to make people sit up and take notice. Whatever the setback, you never knew it. She glowed like the moon. She lived her life believing that you try as hard as possible in any situation—no exceptions. That was what made the difference between success and failure in her eyes. In her desire not to take attention from Camille's wedding with her illness, she tried hard not to be viewed as the dying aunt.

She spent some time on the dance floor with Dad, mostly hugging without much movement. As the night became chilly, she began to tire. The look on her face said it all. Another goal accomplished. She didn't want to focus her time worrying about how much time she had left, but rather leaned on her conviction to succeed.

On the rare times when I could step back and watch her in action, it was truly amazing. Day after day, pound after pound, she seemed to be shedding not just physical weight, but rather emotional weight that had kept her guarded for most of her life. She was finally free of that person; the one that worried about how others perceived her; the one who gave every ounce of her being to those around her at the expense of herself. Like cracking the shell of a nut, she removed the outer layer, allowing her innermost self to be free.

She and I had encountered some amazing people through this journey. Aside from Doctor Reeves, the person that became the most special to us was her palliative nurse, Carly. Knowing firsthand the stress associated with caring for a dying family member, she evoked something inside me that kept me going throughout the process. Knowing all too well what was coming, giving me strength when I needed it most, she seemed to view her time with us as a privilege, helping my sister achieve what was most important to her.

She gave my sister dignity even through the most embarrassing situations. Theresa and I had no secrets, but I still gave her the time alone with Carly in the event she just needed an impartial shoulder to lean on.

Theresa often verbalized how worried she was for my well-being. Knowing I had bonded my life with hers, she feared I would suffer the most when she is gone. Without trying, she had filled a void in me that I never knew was there, revealing strengths I never knew I had. She validated my existence, allowing me to battle something deep inside myself that was begging for liberation. Methodically washed away were my fears of what was to come. I have always believed in the saying, "Something good always comes from something bad," but living with her truly proved it.

Over the next several weeks, her strength continued to lessen as she struggled to consume even soft foods. The tumor continued to squeeze the stomach stent, making it hard to pass any substance and causing tremendous pain.

She battled to keep her life on its course, using most of her strength to overcome nausea, pain, and fatigue. She was in and out of the hospital for the biliary drain, and a new stent placed in the duodenum to help relieve further blocking in the common bile duct. The stent was critical to helping reduce her merciless symptoms.

I wish I could have reassured her that the pain would subside once they placed the new stent in, but that was unrealistic. Adequately controlling her pain would be up to medication now. They upped her Dilaudid and placed her on a low-dose Fentanyl patch. Having an amazing relationship with Doctor Reeves, along with the palliative staff, she could ease into the transition.

The tricky part to a terminal illness is you go through stages of changing your values and what matters most at that current time. Although she wasn't dying as quickly as had been forecasted, this gift was both elating and draining. At one point in time, she insisted on not being out of it because of the medication, but now, she couldn't stay focused through the torment without it.

That evening when Phyllis arrived, she motioned for me to stay while they visited. When a moment of silence presented itself, she blurted out, "While I have you both here, I think, before things get too far, I want to plan my funeral. Annette and I will go there and pick things out, and then I will put it in my trust."

Phyllis sat confused, wondering if there was something we were not telling her. Theresa assured her she wasn't hiding anything, but rather felt things were evolving quickly and time was not on her side. Phyllis looked over at me, hoping to stop the words coming out of her mouth.

She was still fighting. Clearly, she had a lot of life still inside. I didn't think it was the best decision to start planning a final farewell.

"I told you before, you're not planning anything," I insisted. "I've got you covered."

I knew her basic wishes, and I would follow those words when she was gone—lots of laughter, a party with great family and friends, and endless stories that each of us could share about her.

A few weeks prior, I had taken her to the store. She insisted on buying gifts for those closest to her. As she picked out necklaces for each of her sisters, I completely and utterly fell apart, bringing on a tsunami of feelings. I could barely catch my breath. I stepped outside the jewelry store to gain my composure. As I stood staring at her through the glass window, I watched as she laid out each gift for all of us.

A woman passed by me, and then circled back and stood by my side. She was completely unaware of my troubles, but sensed I needed a gentle arm around me. She, too, began to watch Theresa, knowing she was the trigger to my sadness.

"She's pretty incredible, isn't she?" she remarked.

"Yeah, that's my sister," I touted.

Wiping the last tear from my eye, I went back inside to join her. I always stayed strong in her presence, fighting with all my might not to show weakness. However, this time, I couldn't do it. As she sat up straight in her wheelchair, she rubbed her hand against the small of my back.

"You okay?" She knew me well and was upset that she made me cry.

"No worries," I answered. "Just lost it for a minute."

On our way home, we discussed the house she owned. Deciding to sell the rental property was an easy decision for her. She had once shared a life with John and the kids, but now it had no emotional ties and was strictly an investment. Fearing it would cause Phyllis more aggravation after she was gone, she had no trouble deciding to sell it.

Chapter 13

Derek seemed to be around a lot more, insisting on sleeping in the same bed with her, not allowing her to get any sleep. Numerous times we suggested he sleep downstairs to allow her to rest, but he refused. Instead, when she got uncomfortable, he would lie on the floor in the corner of the room, poking his head up like a prairie dog from its hole when I came in and out throughout the night.

He seemed annoyed by my presence, but that was not my concern. For the first time in months, she was calm and relieved from the mountain of pain. She said she felt like he was suffocating her, but I think the reality of losing her scared him. He questioned me about the dosages, as if he needed to protect her from me. She said he didn't understand the increased medications, but clearly he has not witnessed her curled on the edge of the bed, writhing in pain.

My contempt for him grew, and I knew I was just being overprotective at times. But he continued to suck every ounce of extra energy she had inside her to handle his affairs. I couldn't believe a grown man needed to be told to back off and handle his own life. I feared this might be an unwelcome conversation he and I might need to have soon if he didn't wake up.

The conversation to do chemotherapy unexpectedly had come on the forefront once again. I knew her decision to not have treatment had left Derek and her children feeling upset and unable to understand why she wouldn't do anything to stay alive. She truly believed that the treatment was worse than the condition. With no probability of remission, she felt she made the right choice. But the pressure from them drove her to visit the topic once more. She scheduled an appointment with the oncologist at the hospital. This time, we were seen by the guru of chemo, the man patients see when besieged with the most advanced cancers.

I did not question her decision, even though I felt it would be the worst alternative for her care. Arriving early, I parked the car in the basement of the hospital. The damp dim area is something you might see in a scary movie. I think my imagination was getting the best of me. I could see the concern on her face as well. I made light of the day by giving her a wild ride in the wheelchair toward the hospital. Hitting a speed bump, her butt came off the seat. She giggled as I raced through the structure to the sunny outdoors.

Derek was meeting us there to speak to the doctor as well. As we searched to find the office, I noticed several people exiting a building, most of them hairless, either bald or sporting hats. I knew we found our destination.

Doctor Stein came in, a chubby man barely able to close his lab coat. I didn't particularly care for his personality, so maybe that was why I was so judgmental, but there was something inside me that wanted to grab her and run. I knew these doctors were there for a purpose, but I couldn't help but think it was just a witch hunt, looking for their next patient that they can experiment on, hoping to fund their research.

He insisted that she was being foolish for not having treatment and seemed to look toward Derek and me for support. He insisted, "This isn't cheap, so if it didn't work, we wouldn't promote it for the patient." If she even considered treatment, that had to be the worst argument for the cause.

Derek responded with an even more ludicrous assertion, "It's covered by insurance...I hope?" I about fell off my chair. What a stupid statement; like *he* would be the one she would turn to for financial support?

I knew in her heart she didn't want to do this, but the worrying is too much, and she didn't want her children to think she didn't give it her all. Her children viewed their mother as invincible...a warrior...a survivor. Giving into the pressures would be her choice, even though she knew there was no controlling her insatiable cancer.

"Fight—Theresa—fight! I'm getting ready for treatment. I was sad the other night thinking I'm not ready, God. I have to do this for the kids. I committed to fight the monster with chemo. It's funny I wore wigs for years, but the thought of 'having' to wear one bothers me. Not in a bad way, I suppose. I just wish I knew how much this was going to affect me and how much time it will give me—if any."

— From Theresa's Journal

She prepared for chemotherapy. The days leading up she had the stent replaced, and she was still weak from not being able to keep much down because of the nausea. She looked worn and tired.

Carly came to check on Theresa. She cried, knowing this would hurt her rather than help her. Her fears were that this might end her life quicker rather than give her more time, but no one gets that, I guess. I knew she didn't think Theresa had the strength, but for whatever reason, Theresa felt obligated to go through with it.

Carly talked to her about patients that have gone through the treatment, treading lightly. She wanted to tell her don't do it, but there was some code she could not cross. She talked about patients that had treatment. I know those patients have passed away just by the tense in which she referred to them.

Veronica and Clark arrived while Theresa and Carly were talking. They plopped themselves on the couch and turned on the television, talking on their phones and laughing. Clark lay down on the couch texting, while Theresa and Carly were trying to have a serious conversation. Derek showed up as well and didn't step in at all to tell them to give Theresa and Carly some privacy.

Theresa was exhausted, and I could tell she was in no mood to deal with this right now. When Carly left, I told her to go lie down. "You don't need to be the entertainment." When I said that, Derek looked at me stunned like, *Wow, how dare you?*

Phyllis offered to take her to her first chemotherapy session, along with Veronica. Theresa was nervous about them taking her and was worried I wouldn't be there. "Do you think it's okay they take me?"

"Yes, if you are okay with that," I responded.

Phyllis and Veronica were insistent on giving me a break. So Theresa decided to be a big girl and let them take her.

First thing Monday morning, Derek left, but apparently changed his mind and decided to meet them at the hospital.

Phyllis texted me throughout the day with updates. When they got home, Riley and I stood in the garage with the door open, anxiously awaiting their arrival. As I watched her stroll toward me, I could not believe how weak she was. She could barely put one foot in front of the other. If there was an ounce of life left running through her tiny frame, it looked like the chemotherapy stole it. When you spend as much time together as we did, you started to forget how frail she had become. As she went into the house, the doorway appeared to be getting larger as her tiny body barely made an impression.

Phyllis told me that Veronica, Clark, and Derek were so noisy and disruptive during treatment she ended up staying in the waiting room. Theresa's critical condition was bad enough; we didn't need to bring any personal animosity to the table. I guess it made sense that those who are not directly taking care of her would overcompensate for their absence. But their conduct was inappropriate most times, causing unnecessary tensions. I tried so hard to keep a unified family environment, but they made it difficult at times.

I thought the nausea and vomiting was bad prior to treatment, but the chemotherapy had a whole new plan. Riley glued himself to her side as I took her to bed. She slept a lot the next few days. I checked on her often, hoping she was going to make it through this ordeal. She woke up in tremendous pain, primarily because she was unable to keep anything down, throwing up any hopes of the medication that might give her some relief. Facing another day did not seem feasible.

I asked her how she felt about going through the first treatment. "It was a conundrum of emotions," she said. "I was surrounded by people laid back in recliners as the medication coursed through their veins." She continued. "I almost wish I was alone or just with you. The distraction from everyone else was a bit much."

I could tell by her declaration she would have liked to take the time to spend with the other people traveling down similar paths. I think the comradery would have been a powerful thing for her, if she had the chance.

When Carly came to check on her, she could see the marked pain she was experiencing. Additionally, the feeding tube was surrounded once again with granular tissue. Theresa was exhausted and could barely get herself into the bed. Outside the bedroom, Carly expressed to me she might have an infection and suggested we contact Doctor Reeves so he could examine her further.

Early the next morning, we headed to the hospital. The doctor was fully convinced she had an infection and with the chemotherapy only a few days previously, her immune system was, without a doubt, tanked. He communicated his concern about a possible blood clot and decided to admit her for testing. She had no clear screaming symptoms, but his experience told him she was in danger.

Over the next few days, her white blood count continued to drop with an already-pending infection her body would not have the strength to fight off on its own. She was placed on IV antibiotics and a blood culture was taken. Her white count continued to drop to an even more dangerous level. Doctor Reeves decided to up her antibiotics. All the days after that seemed to blur together. Theresa was out of it, barely speaking. She slept most of the time, hardly realizing anyone was there by her side.

Margaret and I feared she wouldn't pull through this. Theresa's biggest fear might be coming to pass. The chemo might kill her rather than give her time. The precious time she had left might be extinguished in the blink of an eye.

The cycle continued until about the fourth day when I arrived that morning. I was greeted by her nurse, and she told me they think she is out of the woods, but she will need to go home with IV antibiotics for the next six weeks.

Doctor Reeves was in the room speaking with her. I decided to take a short walk around the nurses' station to give them some privacy. When I returned, he was gone. I could hear Theresa talking on her phone. She was clearly crying. "You guys need to start realizing things are coming to an end." She continued, "I'm not giving up, but I'm tired. My body is tired, and I'm in so much pain. I'm not sure how much more of this my body can take."

She saw me standing in the hallway and motioned me to come in. "I gotta go," she claimed and hung up the telephone.

Derek texted me the rest of the morning about what was going on with her. He tried to reach her, but she didn't respond. I told him she was getting the picc line this morning so she could go home with the IV antibiotics, and I would keep him posted. She just wanted to be left alone right now with her thoughts, I could sense it. No more worrying about everyone else's needs, at least for today.

She was crying so hard I gave her a hug. She said, "Is Doctor Reeves still out there?" He wasn't. The two of them finally had that heart-to-heart that I saw in his eyes so many times during appointments. She asked if she would make her son's graduation. He told her if it wasn't within the next few months, the likelihood was slim.

As she cried she continued to tell me the conversation. Some people aren't meant for chemo. It made her far too weak and compromised her immune system; the next time she probably wouldn't make it through. Not sure if that is what he said, or that is what she took from their conversation, but either way, no more chemo.

She asked him what was in store for her from this point forward. She worked hard to take the setbacks in stride, and being informed gave her strength. He finally told her the "dwindle" scenario; the same one he had explained to us so many months back. It is so well put that it is effortless to understand, yet its reality is tremendous. I told her he had mentioned that to all of us at the beginning when he couldn't do the surgery. I was sad, and we cried a lot. He told her enjoy each day, and forget all the other people's stuff.

What an amazing person he is. She said over and over, "I wish I had met him under different circumstances." I told her it goes back to the same thing...Something good comes out of something bad, and he was a gift to help you through your toughest moments.

In my heart of hearts, I could not help but wonder why God would bring such a remarkable person into our family's lives while taking our sister from us. In the days that followed, he came in time and time again, and talked to her privately. Whatever he said brought an incredible calm to her.

She told me she had a dream of our grandmother. "She said, 'Theresa, come on; it's time to go.'" She told me how peaceful she felt with the dream, and she was good to go at any time. She knew now that she wouldn't be alone, and Grandma was waiting when she was ready. It scared me when she became so clear about her future; the once-welcome honestly now made me anxious.

The nurse had told me she had awakened her during the evening. Her blood pressure had dropped so low, they had to sit her up in bed to try to regain a normal level. I cannot help but think she might have passed away in the night had the nurses not come in and woke her.

She had done everything that was possible to fight the cancer, but nothing worked. She came to that realization a few months back, but this last encounter made it final. She seemed okay with it, even though she wished she had more time. Her goal from the beginning was making sure her children were set, and now more than ever, this was her only priority.

Theresa had suffered every possible obstacle that pancreatic cancer could throw at her but was still amazingly upbeat. No matter what stumbling blocks she endured, nothing ever dimmed her spirit and determination. She lived life to its fullest, even though most of her days were filled with constant hurdles. From the beginning, her inability to eat would have taken a toll on most people. But she knew aggravating the situation by blending up food concoctions would only make her symptoms worse, so she embraced her tube feedings.

That next day she was discharged and we brought her back to Margaret's house. She was still extremely exhausted and needed to rest. The picc line was in place to administer the antibiotics. With Margaret at the helm, I decided to take the long drive back home to recharge and pick up some things to stay for the week. "I'll be back in a day or so," I told her.

"Come right back," she ordered.

When I got closer to my house I could feel the pressure lifting, and getting home seemed to take forever. I talked to Matt and cried through most of the conversation. He told me I should go back as soon as possible. He could sense my apprehension about coming back home and encouraged me to return the next morning. "Regret is never good," he remarked.

Riley greeted me at the door, looking past me for Theresa. I kneeled and helped him search through my bag for his new toy. He grabbed the stuffed animal and flung it above his head catching it on his back. He put his paws around my neck to give me a big hug, calming my heavy heart.

Theresa texted me all day. "I don't think I can do this without you," she stated. "Margaret is amazing, but I miss you." Her words were gut-wrenching. I didn't sleep much that night fearing I shouldn't have left.

Margaret told me she was wild all day. "You aren't Annette. No offense. But it's not the same."

In one of her texts, she told me it was good I left; she needed her big sister to hug her and take care of her, even though the adjustment was a challenge. I was her security blanket, plain and simple.

Later that night, I checked in with Margaret to see how things were going. She told me Theresa had been crying most of the day. I didn't know if she would make it until I got back. I called Theresa on the phone and told her I would get there first thing in the morning. I encouraged her to take a sleeping pill to rest. She was scared she wouldn't wake up.

"You need your rest," I assured her. "They wouldn't give you something that is going to kill you." She was so overtired; like a child, she needed to be coaxed to sleep.

Sophie decided to make the trip back with me in the morning. When we arrived, Theresa had heavy bags under her eyes, but she was perky and refreshed. The last week had been filled with lots of tears, restless sleep, and copious amounts of drugs running through her system.

Having her hair and makeup done was always a crucial element for her. She didn't want to appear as "the patient."

Nothing over the top...Just enough to show she cared about her appearance.

A friend from her work was going to stop by that afternoon so she wanted to look presentable. She had such a tremendous acknowledgment for people around her and their feelings. She never wanted anyone to feel uncomfortable in her presence. Especially those from her past. Sarah would be no different. She and Theresa had been friends for several years, with the same, unwavering work ethic. Theresa had told me the year prior, Sarah had lost her sister to cancer, so the feeling of losing someone close was fresh to her.

She was a spiritual woman and told Theresa that her church had her in their prayers. This made her a bit uneasy. I think she felt, over the last few months, she had logged in enough hours on her own; God had answered, not perhaps what she had hoped for, but she knew He had a purpose for her, and that kept her grounded.

Sarah had brought a prayer bear for Theresa. Something that was to bring her comfort and peace of mind during difficult times. But for her, it was a source of angst. She held the bear tightly while Sarah visited, but asked me to put it in the other room later that night. Over the next few days, she would question me about the bear's whereabouts. I assured her it was in a safe place, but she wanted to know exactly where.

"Why?" I inquired.

"There is so much energy coming from that bear I can feel its presence," she claimed. I never did understand what her infatuation with the bear was, but whatever the reason, it bothered her. So I tried not to joke about it.

Together, we seemed to find humor in everything. That next morning in the glistening sun, the peach fuzz on my face became the topic of conversation. I was towheaded as a child;

my hair remained relatively light as I got older. The hair on my face never seemed to bother me, but apparently, Margaret felt it needed to come off. She insisted on breaking out the Epilady that she fondly called the "beard mower."

With tool in hand, she guided me to the bathroom and showed me how to use the device. As the hair was being painstakingly ripped from my cheeks, I screeched in pain. Theresa stood in the bathroom doorway laughing. "I am not doing this," I claimed. "No sane person would put a twirling hair ripper on their face and consider this a good thing." Theresa held her side laughing as Margaret continued with her instructions.

"Give me that thing," Theresa insisted.

She grabbed the footstool in the corner of the bathroom and instructed me to sit down. As I sat perched below her on the stool, she held my forehead back with one hand while working the trimmer with the other. I shrieked in horror as she continued. "Hold still or you might lose something you want." I could hear Margaret and Sophie in the kitchen hooting violently as I sat in Theresa's house of torture, while she held me in a headlock.

When the laughter died down, we sat in the kitchen cackling about the morning. Theresa broke the laughter with a heavier subject. She told us she isn't giving up, but the end is nearing, and she has decided to be cremated. Originally, she was going to be buried in my parents' crypt but decided against it.

"I can't be alone with those two in the crypt," she insisted. "I need to be with everyone."

Raised Catholic, it was always believed that you should be buried beneath the grass, giving the power for those who are left behind to bond with your remains. But for her, she wanted to be everywhere and a piece of her with everyone. I felt the same. I'd rather she be in an urn on my counter than in a lonely graveyard surrounded by strangers. As time passed, most people only visit their loved ones on special occasions. In time, people move away or their life takes different paths, and then the grave site becomes just a place where your loved one is kept.

Wanting to see friends from work and those she had not seen since she moved, we decided to plan a luncheon; it just seemed fitting as Theresa felt time for her was slipping away. Why wait to have people come visit her on her deathbed? Why not have a party when she could still enjoy their company? One of her biggest requests to me was she didn't want people staring at her while she slept or was too sick to be conscious of her surroundings. For some reason, that, above all, made her very uneasy. She made me promise that when she was close to dying, it should just be her and I. No one crying and no one watching her as she struggled to take those last few breaths.

No doubt, some people would opt not to come because of their own fears or perhaps thinking they had plenty of time to visit. I cannot help but think our minds do it as a defense mechanism, rather than facing what is sure to come. Besides, I knew this would be far more fun than friends at a funeral; at least Theresa would be present.

Randy was threatening to make an appearance, which might cause a bit of tension because Derek would be there as well. But Theresa didn't care; she wanted to see everyone and share stories with those from her not-so-distant past.

That afternoon while planning the event, she called me to the bedroom in a panic. The human resources department at her work failed to tell her that her medical benefits were ending, and she would need to pay her own premiums through a Cobra plan or her coverage would be terminated. I sprang into action and made the necessary telephone calls and paid her coverage to avoid a lapse. The cruel reality of life is, while you are struggling to live the last bit of time you have on earth, you are still faced with the never-ending challenges of life.

That afternoon before the party, I helped her shower and get herself ready for her friends. She casually came out of the bathroom with a large clump of hair grasped in her fist. "I guess the hair is going too," she remarked.

"Just pile on the hairspray and don't mess with it." I instructed. "It'll stay in place at least until after the party."

Doctor Reeves called to see how she was feeling. When she hung up, she told us he told her he only wished he could have done more for her. I could see the sadness in her eyes; not for herself but for him.

"He has given me life; he has given me strength. I feel so bad that he thinks he somehow failed me." He told her that her strength and determination had given her this extra time, and she should be proud of herself.

The party was a huge success. It helped her forget what she was facing and appreciate where she had been. She appreciated the emotional strength it must have taken for each person to come and spend that time with her. I think it gave her spirit motivation to continue the battle. She expressed her biggest fear of people coming to pay their so-called respects and break down in tears as they said their good-byes.

Her slender frame was a far cry from how they once knew her. However, it allowed her to wear clothes she never thought were possible for her once-chunky size. She took that opportunity to live it up in her new body that would soon be unrecognizable to all of us, including herself.

The festivities were filled with reminiscences and laughter; any thoughts of what was to come for her wasn't mentioned. She was the glue in most relationships and was moving toward her death in the same fashion she embraced in life... with control and certainty, saying what she wanted to say while she still had the chance.

Although Theresa wore wigs out of preference because she had always thought her hair was unruly, it was part of who she was. Now, all that's left of her own hair were a few scraps on her scalp and a waste basket filled with what once was.

The next morning, we summoned Hank to break out the hair clippers to give Theresa a proper haircut. Without hesitation, he went to the back bathroom and emerged with the shears. As he ran the blade front to back, she sat calmly and confidently, embracing the next phase of her condition. When he was done, she ran both hands back and forth across her head. "It feels so strangely liberating," she said.

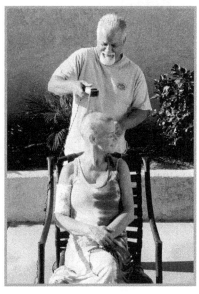

She looked so cute, and her perfectly shaped head embraced its newfound freedom.

After lots of pictures, Margaret came out with these ridiculous hairpieces. Theresa put them on her head and posed. She was now in her long, silk nightgown; she looked like she was going to prom.

After an hour or so, she crashed from all the fun. I lay at the foot of the bed talking to her as she dozed off, thinking I wouldn't have changed these times for anything. I told Margaret and Sophie, "She looks amazing, and her spirit is so full of life. It's hard to believe that she is truly sick." Saying it out loud almost seemed wrong, she was so at peace with herself. I cannot explain it; it is as if this were a gift rather than a curse.

Chapter 14

Christopher headed back to college. She assured him it was the right thing to do, knowing each time he left might be the last time he would see his mother. She stayed strong for him and tried hard not to break down in front of him. Her only worry was that he wouldn't finish college, something they worked together to achieve, and an important part of her legacy.

With his graduation more than a year away, she knew her fast-moving cancer wouldn't allow her to see him finish. Theresa told me that every time he left, her chest was so heavy and her heart pounded for him. "I feel like I swallowed a jawbreaker," she told me. "The lump in my throat cannot be cleared as I fight with the thousand tears threatening to spill out of my eyes."

She told us she was heartbroken that she wouldn't be able to finish their goal together, feeling like she was abandoning him, even though she knew she couldn't control her destiny. The death of his mother was right around the corner. She only hoped the delay of the inevitable would be long enough for him to prepare himself for life without her. She knew she would be left out of one of the most important events of her son's life; the son she cherished and loved so much and would be experiencing one of the best things in his life without her.

She tried her hardest not to be an emotional cripple. She didn't want to waste precious time focusing on his departure and the inescapable send-off, but rather embracing each precious moment she could have with him.

Riley sensed her apprehension of letting her son leave one more time. He stayed close to Theresa's side, giving her the comfort and strength she needed to hold it together.

Christopher stayed strong for his mom. No matter what he was feeling inside, he didn't give her any reason to be concerned about him. "I'll see you at Christmas," he claimed. "I love you, Momma."

Derek didn't want to grasp what was going on around him, giving me the impression he was only concerned about how her condition was impacting his life. Theresa was always worrying about everyone else, leaving her needs unattended. He seemed only to annoy her. Despite her words of endearment, I could not help but think she was just going through the motions. Perhaps it was because he had seen her at her most vulnerable times, or maybe intimate secrets only he was privy to; something she was ashamed to reveal. I could only presume I didn't know this side of her; the side she kept away from those who knew her best—her sisters.

Meanwhile, Veronica was moving forward with her wedding plans. Despite Theresa's clear reluctance for her to marry Clark, she pushed through for her mom to handle the details of the wedding. Suddenly, now every moment Theresa was awake, she spent ordering and making decisions for the wedding.

Veronica and Clark had decided on a wedding on a yacht at the marina only a few days after Christmas. I didn't think Theresa would be able to handle the journey to the wedding, and being out on a boat for four hours didn't seem like a good option for her health. Not to mention Christmas was a few months off, and I wasn't sure Theresa had the endurance to live that long. She tried to explain this to Veronica, but her face said it all. Annoyed that she couldn't have her way, she insisted the wedding wouldn't be what she wanted.

Initially, it was all about getting married while her mom would be able to attend. But, clearly, that wasn't the motive. She wanted it her way and she would make Theresa's life miserable until she conceded. The few days of pouting and silence from Veronica gave Theresa the opportunity to find a venue that could suit everything. A gorgeous hilltop location at an exclusive golf course in our area would prove to be her final decision.

That afternoon, Veronica broke her silence and came by the house. Theresa informed her they had an appointment with the event planner to go over the menu and the details of the affair. Although Veronica was annoyed, she could see her mother had made up her mind and agreed to go with us to see the location.

Theresa and I had many conversations about the wedding, and she was clear she didn't think Clark could take care of Veronica. "Veronica is struggling and has become someone I don't recognize," she said. "I think Veronica believes she'll never find someone else."

Theresa's biggest fear above all was that she believed he was using drugs again. His weight had dropped significantly, and she was amazed her daughter just didn't see it. "I love her, and this breaks my heart," she continued. "But I can't stress about it anymore. I don't have the energy. I can only pray."

Theresa made a mental bucket list. She admitted she held a few things back, recognizing that when the checklist was complete, she, too, would be done. "I know myself. When everything I want to accomplish is done, I'll be able to let go." She was painfully aware that there was so much truth to what she said.

Theresa was visibly tired and suffering now. It seemed like time was no longer on her side. The other night she came down to the kitchen. Matt and I were standing at the counter. I had only seen her an hour or so earlier. When I glanced at her, I thought, *Wow, this is it.* Theresa surprised me now every day when she awoke. I was expecting her to be gone each day, yet she still plugged along.

Theresa insisted there was a smell coming from her body, a damp, waning odor. "You are just close to the drains," I insisted. "I can't smell anything."

Yes, I had noticed a strange odor, too. Usually in the morning, after her door had been closed for the night, it was much more apparent. I sprayed and washed sheets and blankets, but each day, it was the same smell. Sort of a sweet, rotting fruit smell, I guess. She was always clean and showered, so I couldn't imagine what it could be, but there it was, following us. The cancer smell was following us.

I had a ritual in her room each morning. I would wait until she was awake and moving about doing her daily routine, then I would strip her bed every other day and spray with an antibacterial spray on the days in between. When I came into her room that morning, I began straightening the room and intensely spraying the top of her blankets. Something moving beneath the covers startled me. Her eyes peeked out over the blankets, and suddenly, I realized Theresa was beneath them.

"What are you doing?" She coughed and snickered in the same breath. "I'm still in here."

Growing up, my side of the room was a complete pigpen. My tolerance level for messiness was high. Most days, my side of the room looked like we had been robbed—clothes strewn everywhere, books scattered across the floor, my Catholic school uniform not ironed and rumpled in the corner of the closet. The only time I cleaned up was when Mom would get so fed up, she would dump everything I owned in the center of my bed and forced me to clean it all up before I could go out and play.

As I grew up and had my own place, something changed. I turned into Felix Unger from the television show, *The Odd Couple*. Obsessively neat, floors scrubbed clean with bleach, and everything in its proper place; lucky for me, my husband appreciated my obsession.

My family was in shock most of the time, remembering my younger years and wondering what happened. They call me a germophobe, but I don't care. When Theresa came to stay with me, I would make people take off their shoes before going upstairs to visit. Any telltale sign of a snot-bubble and they couldn't visit. I know Theresa appreciated my craziness, but teased me just the same.

"When I'm gone, I'm going to leave fingerprints on your walls," she declared. "Just to torture you."

She had mentioned the smell to Doctor Reeves, but he never seemed to react to the question. I'm sure he knew the cancer smell all too well. From the onset, she said she smelled, but I chalked it up to the dreadful stink that emanated when she emptied the biliary bag. I figured the smell had embedded in her nostrils over time.

With all the mayhem surrounding the wedding plans, we decided to escape to Margaret's house for a few days. Theresa told Derek this was a girl's trip and she would see him next weekend. Sophie came as well, and we spent the day talking. Theresa had been crying a lot these last few weeks, almost to her frustration. "This crying is making me crazy . . . I cry about everything and nothing. I cannot get my fight back."

That night, I saw one of my ghost friends again. I always centered my thoughts on Theresa's will to live, but now my mind seemed aimed at the reality that she was ready to die. The feeling was so overwhelming, I had to get my mind away from it; it was making me paranoid. Theresa had been having many visitors—all from people who were no longer among the living. She spoke about it as if it was the next transition for her passage. She felt comfort knowing that as she inched closer to the end, there were loved ones ready to guide her through the process.

It was nice being able to put all the bullshit at home aside. I wanted her to be peaceful and happy for these last days—no stress, no drama, just great times with her sisters. Her pale skin had become sallow, perhaps from the extreme pain she was having trouble getting in front of.

She rested most of the day. When she emerged, she was clearly struggling in excruciating agony. I escorted her to the couch to lie down. She curled in a ball, grasping a blanket with her chin tucked in tight to her chest. "I think I need to see Doctor Reeves."

When we arrived, staff swiftly took her back to an emergency room bay. All too familiar was this environment.

Doctor Reeves was in surgery all afternoon, so he had one of the other doctors meet her. He was young and handsome; someone Theresa might have liked the attention from if she wasn't in so much pain. They ran some lab tests and decided to admit her for the evening. Our girls' weekend had now turned into a stay at the hospital.

I heard Doctor Reeves speaking in the hallway. He fondly talked about another patient, and then he came into the room, wearing a blue hat and scrubs.

"What's going on, little lady?"

"Not feeling so great," she replied.

He questioned her about the other doctor, making sure he lived up to his expectations. He asked tactfully so you hardly noticed his inquisition. As he examined Theresa, she expressed her concern about the odor. He told her he was not necessarily sure it was an infection, but rather necrotic tissue sluffing off from the tumor.

"I want to keep you here and make sure another infection isn't getting the best of you," he said. He told her he would be gone for the next few days, but his partner, Doctor Vaughn, would take care of her until he returned. "You're in good hands," he vowed. "Going to see my parents." He smiled. He told us his parents were ninety-three years old, and he was going on a quick visit. Makes you wonder if the vegetarian life he grew up on was the driving force that kept his parents so vibrant.

As suspected, she did have an infection. They started her on IV antibiotics and addressed the other major issue: her constipation. On top of everything else, this was a constant battle for her. You would think with only taking in liquids this would not be an issue, but it was, constantly. She was so nauseated and struggled to keep anything down. They ordered a steady flow of GoLYTELY administered through her feeding tube. She was relieved they had found another option. The last time they tried to make her drink it, she struggled not to vomit all over the bathroom floor while trying to choke down the horrendous potion. They claimed the flavor packet helped with the taste, but she asserted it was nothing short of salty toilet water.

Theresa spiked a fever a few hours after the flushing ordeal. She was tired, but finally settled and was able to rest after numerous trips to the bathroom. They upped her Fentanyl patch, along with the Dilaudid, so she was finally relaxed. She laid her head to the side of the bed, talking to me, as she dozed in and out of sleep.

"Do you think Doctor Reeves is pulling away from me?"

"What would give you that idea?"

"I don't know, but I would totally understand. He knows our relationship is coming to an end."

I shook my head. "You're nuts."

I felt so bad for her. He was such a big part of her life. I think she was sad she was going to have to let him go at some point. I think it helped her to talk about everything. I guess once you say it enough times, you train yourself to be numb to the shock.

She always felt this overwhelming belief to stay strong. She grew to hate the cliché, "Live each day as if it is your last." It didn't make sense now that she was truly facing death. Rather, she told me several times that if she was happy and the people around her were happy, she was doing something right.

Derek decided to make a trip to the hospital. She was extremely agitated when he arrived. I was not sure if it was his presence or perhaps the telephone call she had with him a few hours prior. When she talked to him earlier, I could tell by her face he was whining about something. It was amazing to me still at this stage of the game he didn't even attempt to hide his problems. Instead, he brought them front and center to her attention.

"Crazy, deal with it . . . What will you do when she's gone?" I asserted.

When Doctor Reeves returned, he decided to check the positioning of her feeding tube in outpatient surgery. With all the commotion of the last few days, the hose kept trying to creep out. He assured her he didn't think there was a problem, but he only wanted to make sure before he let her go home.

While awaiting someone to bring her to outpatient surgery, Derek sat quietly and didn't say anything. Theresa was still in tremendous pain, despite all the medication. As she shuffled in the bed to get comfortable and kicked the blankets off her legs, I glanced over at him, and I caught him rolling his eyes at her. I could not believe he could be that heartless. No compassion at all for the pain and torture she seemed now destined to constantly bear. He looked down at his phone and hoped I didn't notice.

When the orderly arrived, Derek stayed behind in her room. Margaret and I followed behind the gurney as we navigated down some back corridors to an elevator taking us to the fourth floor.

When we arrived at outpatient surgery, Keith, a male nurse that treated Theresa many times prior, greeted us. We encountered many special people along the way. He was one of them. His tall frame engulfed her as he gave her a big hug. "Great to see you, girl."

Cautiously optimistic that the infection was under control, she was able to leave. Later that night, she told me she was ready to go back home in the morning.

Tomorrow was Halloween. She and Matt had been avidly speaking about pumpkin carving for weeks. In the morning, I looked out the window to see the wind whipping the trees back and forth. No matter how still the night before was, Halloween always seemed turbulent.

I peeked in to check on Theresa. Surprisingly, she was awake and packing her bag. "I'm ready when you are," she claimed.

I should never be surprised with her strength because somehow, she always managed to amaze me. Her eyes were bright and her pale face now held color. She put on a cute orange shirt and her favorite bracelet and leggings that were barely filled out now with her tiny frame.

"You ready?" she asked. "All the pumpkins are going to be gone."

I dashed back to the bedroom and put my things together. Then I leaned my head into the hallway and shouted to Margaret, startling her as she rounded the corner. "I guess we're going." We both giggled, knowing when Theresa was ready, you better be standing at attention. "And she calls *me* bossy?" I claimed.

When we got home, Matt and Riley were sitting out front, anxiously awaiting our arrival. Theresa loved the holidays, and Matt, too, was a big kid when they came around, so it was fun to see her so happy to do something she truly looked forward to doing.

Riley fought her for position in the front seat, standing on the console with his paw on her shoulder, watching through the windshield, as we drove the short distance to the farm. When I glanced over, I saw her smile at him, as if they shared a private language. She had laughed hard, loved long, and taught us all a valuable lesson in life; he got it. He understood her, and as sad as I know he will be when she was gone, he would be happy her soul was set free.

When we got to the fields, the pumpkins seemed endless. For a magical hour, she was no longer chronically ill. She laughed and pointed out all her favorite gourds in the patch. The owner gave us a wagon to put all our treasures in, which she decided to sit in so I could pull her around. It was as if, for that brief time, the cancer curse had been broken. Her adrenaline rushed through her as we laughed like kids. All in all, we ended up with *eight* huge pumpkins. Ten seemed too many and five not enough.

We feverishly tried on Halloween costumes while Riley and Matt watched our fashion show. I fell over in the hay while maneuvering in my Foghorn Leghorn getup. She skipped past the merry-go-round, sporting a *Wizard of Oz* Dorothy wig and slippers. I plodded through the sawdust, flopping around in my big rooster feet and giggling uncontrollably as Matt laughed and Riley barked his approval.

When we got back to the house, I spread newspaper out on the picnic table in the yard; Theresa and I began the challenge. Matt keenly decided on his design. James showed up not long after and grabbed his favorite jack-o'-lantern, painfully planning his creation. With what seemed like hours of feverishly cutting with our plastic utensils, we each finally finished our works of art. I adorned each with a candle and placed them at the front door.

"I know nobody will read my status [Facebook]*, but sometimes when I'm bored, I get wrapped up in my tiny tutu, put a giant horn on my head, lather sparkles all over myself, and prance around the kitchen, pretending I am a magical unicorn."*

— From Theresa's Journal

The rush had worn off. Theresa was exhausted, but so truly happy. She always managed to pull herself up by the bootstraps. Even though her life was collapsing around her, she found the energy to enjoy even the simplest things.

Derek arrived when we were done, late as usual. I elected not to quash my happiness with his presence, so I decided to take Riley for a walk around the park. As I thought about the last week with her, I couldn't help but feel proud to have her as my sister. She met her fate with brave quietness. She was a fighter, not a victim of cancer; that would have been harsh for most people to assimilate.

I stopped periodically and hugged Riley. He brought me such comfort on an almost unbearable path I was on with Theresa. He looked up at me with a smile. I knew he felt my pain. He had saved me from so many challenging days when I thought I would crack under the pressure.

When I arrived back home, Theresa was awake, and her energy seemed restored. I was surprised that Derek had left while I was gone.

"Where'd he go?" I inquired.

"He was whining, so I told him, 'If you can't come here without a mountain of problems, you need to take your happy ass home.'" She shrugged. "That's it. I need a break."

Her tolerance for the never-ending bullshit appeared to be at a breaking point. She had liberated herself once before from the burden of supporting a maladjusted partner through life, and it was now clear she didn't want him to continue to warp her happiness with his drama.

Theresa always knew how to dominate the room. One minute she could blow up and scream like a maniac, but five minutes later, all was back to normal. She didn't have the time or the inclination to stay mad at someone; holding a grudge was not her thing. She would rather let off some steam and get it over with, allowing herself to move forward. Her ejection of Derek was no different. She was not going to allow him to delegate her time to all his problems when she was having such an amazing day.

That night she was up until the early morning hours. I checked on her around 3:00 a.m. and she was still lying in bed, playing a game on her phone and posting pictures of our pumpkin carvings on Facebook.

She had rekindled some old relationships that she had long put behind her. She allowed people into her life that she had let go long ago. The relationships that had become distant, and whatever had caused her separation from them, were now long forgotten. People who had learned of her condition and perhaps wanted to right a wrong were contacting her.

She realized in her short life she had been through many ups and downs like most of us. "What could they do to me now?" she insisted. "I've been made fun of, I've been ridiculed, I've been broke and almost on the streets. No one can take away my spirit now. Not even this cancer." Welcoming those from her past seemed like the right thing to do.

Theresa had spent her whole life boldly living up to her own expectations, doing things that she wasn't always mentally equipped to do. But, somehow, she pulled them off. She wanted Veronica to enforce her strengths as well, realizing she could do anything she set her mind to, always trying to build her self-confidence. However, Veronica seemed determined to live the simple life with Clark.

The wedding was shaping up to be amazing, and Theresa was proud she could give her daughter this one last wish. She decided she wasn't going to fight it any longer. She only hoped there would come a day when Veronica would remember her mother's powerful words and perhaps make a better life for herself. For now, however, she was going to give in to her daughter's request and give her an extraordinary wedding.

Chapter 15

The next week was like the stock market crash of the 1980s; Theresa's stock was plummeting. She was tired, worn out and unable to get out of pain. Carly came for a visit and remarked that her blood pressure was extremely low. This compounded her pain because I had to hold off on giving her any medication until her blood pressure stabilized.

"Something is wrong," she claimed. "I can feel that something is wrong."

Carly tried to narrow down what she was feeling, but Theresa insisted she just wasn't "right." She was experiencing a severe headache, a symptom she hadn't previously encountered. The unrelenting pain subsided once we could give her an Ativan followed by Dilaudid. Still, she insisted there was something hiding in the background.

Despite her fears of the dark, there was one special person she looked forward to seeing time and again. She took solace in the fact that my grandmother had come to visit her on several occasions. She began sleeping with the bathroom light on, which I was not sure if it was out of a phobia of the night, or perhaps to get a clearer look at her visitor.

I climbed into the bed next to my sister and asked her if she wanted to go see Doctor Reeves.

"I don't want to keep bothering him, but something is different. I feel so weird."

"Well, then, let's go."

I could see she was growing weary, but continued to forge on for the sake of her daughter's wedding. As dusk came, we jumped in the car and headed to Margaret's house for the night. We had an appointment to see Doctor Reeves in the morning.

"I'm sorry," she said. "I just get nervous at times."

She had been feeling excessive lower abdominal pain, which was something new, and feared she might be heading for a bowel obstruction, something she had been all too mindful of; with her condition, it was likely imminent.

She slept most of the way, waking periodically, and then falling back to sleep. The medication had kicked in, and she was finally calm. I was so worried for her safety, but also tired from my own sleepless nights. I hadn't eaten, and the jumbo soda I drank only added to my jitters. I felt almost drugged as the headlights from the horrendous traffic glared in my eyes. By the time we reached Margaret's house, I had a splitting headache. I just wanted to lie down and rest.

When we arrived, we both went straight to bed. The house was quiet and peaceful; the blast of the heater felt good against my cold body. I tried to fall asleep, but my anxiety was getting the best of me. I lay in bed with my eyes closed, hoping the migraine would pass. I heard Theresa throughout the night, in and out of the bathroom. I checked on her a few times. She said she just had a lot of pressure in her pelvic area.

"It's like the worst menstrual cramps ever," she explained.

"Maybe you're pregnant, Sprouts."

"Yeah, Immaculate Conception." She giggled, holding her side. "I won't be Sprouts much longer, my hair is growing back."

❧ ❧ ❧

Doctor Reeves smiled and shook our hands as he entered the exam room. "The girls are back," he said.

He talked to Theresa calmly as he cauterized the tissue escaping from her feeding tube site. She winced in pain. He apologized, but continued, suspecting an infection and ordered lab tests. She told him the antibiotic he gave her last time in the hospital made her feel good.

With emphasis, she said, "*Reaaaaaally* good."

He told her he could admit her.

"Veronica's shower is this weekend," she informed him. "I cannot miss that."

"We can work this out," he assured her and set her up for infusion therapy for the next three days.

He ordered a CT scan to find out what was causing the lower abdominal pain, which, fortunately, was only a small pelvic mass, most likely an ovarian cyst that was causing most of the pain. He spoke with the gynecology department, and they said they could perform a transvaginal ultrasound as well. However, it wasn't a bowel obstruction. Doctor Reeves was relieved and didn't feel putting her through any more tests was necessary.

Nevertheless, she was constipated once again, and with a looming infection that her labs confirmed, he admitted her for IV antibiotics and a cycle of GoLYTELY. Curled in a ball, she wished for nauseousness to pass, with the pink bucket positioned next to her face. She lay still waiting for the Zofran to provide some relief.

That evening, once things quieted down, she asked for a sleeping pill, hoping to sleep through the storm of pain. However, the nurse couldn't give it to her; her blood pressure, once again, was dangerously low, so she couldn't take the chance.

I decided to stay the night with her. I knew things were getting closer. She just had a way about her I could not describe. She was always giving me updates on the things she had taken care of. Her eyes seemed glazed, or maybe I was just imagining things. I knew it was nearing, but she held on tight to handle the things she thought were important, but feeling less and less able. Unfortunately, that was not in her hands, but rather in God's hands. I only hoped she could pass calmly without any medical incident.

Sitting up in bed, she lifted her head and patted it lightly, as if in deep thought. "I need to make it to the wedding."

Her pain was a constant reminder of her approaching mortality. I could sense she knew she didn't have long. Each time she had another infection or a new symptom, it resonated like a ticking time bomb through her thoughts. She worried she might ruin her daughter's wedding day because of her now-fragile condition. I assured her that was nothing further from the truth. If she made it, everything would fall in its place, and it would be amazing.

She worried she would become a huge burden for me to take care of her. I told her time and time again, I could handle everything and for her not to worry, but it sat in the back of her mind. She lay in bed, looking up at the ceiling, as we spoke.

"I'm going to die in your house; you know, right? If you ever sell your place, you'll have to disclose that."

"What? Are you a real estate agent, now? You stew about the craziest things." I insisted she had plenty of time to worry about other things and not to concern herself with such nonsense.

Life wasn't fair. I would soon be losing my sister, my friend. For both of us, laughter gave us fuel to keep going— she to fight for her life, and me to keep her happy until the very end. I continued to talk until she dozed off to sleep. There would be no unfinished business for her. I made a promise to myself I would do whatever it took to fill her last days with happiness.

Lying in a fetal position, she finally was fast asleep. Her back was visible through her hospital gown. It amazed me how she kept going in her frail condition. She was so thin; her once-beefy back was now just bones covered by skin. She looked like an X-ray. I could see each vertebra, one after the other. Her skull was almost visible in the back of her head.

Theresa's eating was undoubtedly getting less and less. She tried, but was unable to force herself to eat. She was only tube feeding about five hundred calories per day, at best. She hadn't fed now in two nights. Neither I, nor the nursing staff, were forcing her. Whatever she wanted now at this point was what we would do. She drank chicken broth, water, and an occasional Jell-O, but that was all by mouth.

Friday morning came quickly, and the nurse signed us out of the hospital. The hospital staff had become all too familiar to us.

"Where's the other sister?" the nurse inquired.

"We made her fetch the car," I joked, as I escorted Theresa down the elevator and through the lobby in a wheelchair.

Theresa got out of the wheelchair and sat next to me on the cement planter while we waited for Margaret to bring the car around. Her eyes began to water, and she covered her face with her shirt.

"Hang in there," I told her.

Theresa was glad she was going to make it to the shower, but it was short-lived. "I have lost my edge," she claimed. "I'm trying so hard to stay focused on the people around me and the things I should be excited about, but I just don't seem to care, and that makes me sad." She saw Margaret pulling the car up to the front. "Here she comes. I need to stop crying." Theresa fanned her hands in front of her face.

I put my arm around her. "I've got this."

The wedding shower was amazing. Theresa looked stunning and played off her condition as if nothing was wrong. She and Veronica took several pictures with the guests. As I glanced at each photo on my phone, they all had one common factor. With the ashen sunburst through the windows of the restaurant, a lustrous light beamed behind Theresa's head in each photo. No matter where she stood in the restaurant, the light seemed to follow. It were as if someone were standing over her shoulder, guiding her and helping her get through yet another memorable day.

As the day moved forward, I glanced over at Theresa sitting in a booth in the corner of the room. I could see she was crashing. Today was a lot, both emotionally and physically; the overpowering adrenaline rush was wearing off, and her body began to shiver. I could tell by the look on her face it was time to go home.

She said some quick goodbyes to the remaining guests and tried to exit without causing too much commotion. Once

in the car, I wrapped her tightly in a blanket like a baby in a papoose. Neither of us said much on the ride back to the house, which happened often. I guess that was all the years of spending so much time together, we sensed what the other was thinking. She was convinced that she truly made her daughter happy, and everything was falling into place, as it should be.

When we got back to the house, she climbed into bed. I gave her the beanie that Veronica had knitted for her to try to warm her further. Her body was still mildly shivering, which seemed to go away once she relaxed. They had recently increased her medications to keep in front of the pain. She was afraid again to take the sleeping pill, sure she wouldn't wake up.

"It is early in the morning; everyone is asleep, but not me. It hurts to lie down; my body is so numb, the numb hurts. I wish I could hide this fear and sadness so no one sees. I think I see why people leave with this monster disease so fast; it is hard feeling yourself fade. I look in the mirror and wonder who is looking back at me. Who is this bony, fragile, wracked-with-pain woman that still tries to make others feel okay? I feel almost guilty telling people I feel like crap."

— From Theresa's Journal

Derek never made it out for the weekend, which didn't upset me much. He didn't like that they upped her pain medication. He and Theresa got into a heated discussion about it earlier that morning. However, he wasn't the one that had to watch her day after day coiled in a ball from the unyielding pain. She claimed he was just worried about the higher dosages, but I think it was because he couldn't manipulate her in her altered cognitive state.

She slept almost the whole next day. Phyllis sent me a text about coming by for a visit. She claimed she had tried to text and call Theresa most of the afternoon, but never received a response. I insisted that she had just been resting and perhaps didn't hear her phone, but I knew different. Theresa had become less and less interested in anyone or anything, apart from me. I had heard that same comment, quite frequently, from everyone close to her. The phone that she always kept by her side to play games on or talk to people was now no longer important.

When Phyllis arrived, I told her to just text or call me from this point forward. Theresa was in an emotional fog of sorts, I claimed. As she checked off each event on her list, she became more and more at peace within herself. Tranquility now replaced the heavy sadness. The desire to hold on to things that used to be crucial had passed. She was now finding internal quiet.

My part, from this point forward, was to stay strong for her. I needed to be the rock she once was. I needed to be even-keeled and keep my emotions to myself, staying strong for those close to her. I have always been a very logical person, and this situation was no different. It was vital now for me to reboot my brain. Deep inside me, I needed to burry the encompassing shattering grief that I felt as I watched my sister dying.

Her biliary drain had partially slipped out, so our time home was short-lived. I couldn't help but wonder why God had chosen to keep her here so long. Was it the fight instilled in her from birth or perhaps a message for her and our family? I believe she had been on this earth before. Perhaps there was unfinished business that this process would finally free her soul for eternity.

"When I'm gone, I won't be back any time soon," she claimed. "I think I need a rest from this earth."

Everything in her life seemed like such an uphill battle, with all the stress resting firmly on her shoulders. If we do have control of coming back to this earth, I completely understood why she would want to stay in heaven.

I sat in the waiting area while they replaced the drain. It seemed to be taking an unusually long time; I began to get a little nervous. As I glanced in the direction of where the doctor usually emerged, the double doors swung open and a nurse walked toward me. As the doors began to close behind her, I saw Theresa standing there, looking toward me, wearing her nightgown and tie-dyed T-shirt she always wore to bed. At that moment, I thought something must have happened. Her soul had come to say goodbye. It gave me chills. I thought this was it. I closed my eyes tightly, and then opened them slowly. She was gone.

"She's in recovery," the nurse claimed. "I can take you back there to sit with her."

It took me a second to process what she was saying. I jumped up from my chair and followed behind her, but I couldn't shake the emotional feeling that I thought I had just lost her.

Doctor Reeves came in and gave us the thumbs-up to go home. "I want to see you tomorrow before you head back home," he insisted.

It was late afternoon. I ran to get the car while she waited inside. It had begun to rain quite hard. I gave her my hooded sweatshirt to cover her bald head and escorted her fragile body into the front seat. She kept saying how tired she was. I'm not sure if she was talking to me or just speaking her thoughts aloud. We had gotten an unusual amount of rain this season. I began to think every time the clouds would roll in the angels were coming to give her a ride to heaven.

Once back at Margaret's house, she went straight to the couch to lie down. She fell asleep so quickly I almost thought she was joking with me. Margaret hadn't arrived home from work yet, so I sat quietly on the patio as the rain continued to teem down off the roof. I wanted to be by her side when she finally goes. I knew that seemed morose, but I needed to see her take her last breath. We have been by each other's side throughout it all, and I knew when she was gone, a piece of me would leave with her.

I could not get the appearance of her behind the nurse from my mind. It seemed like it was an out-of-body experience for her. My nerves were shot today. When Margaret arrived home, she tiptoed past Theresa and joined me on the patio. I told her about my vision. I told her how real it felt, as if I could reach out and touch her.

Not long after, Theresa woke up and came outside to sit with us. It was unusually warm, considering the heavy rainstorm, but we opted to go inside so Theresa didn't catch a cold. She tried hard to focus on the conversation, but the pain was clearly intense.

"I'm not sure if I need to even see Doctor Reeves tomorrow," she claimed. "I think it's time to let him off the hook." She gave a courageous smile.

I knew he had grown so fond of her. She had that effect on people. Their relationship was special. I think he somehow felt guilty for not being able to help her. Yet, he did help her more than he will ever realize. I think she had a lot of unfinished business in her life, and this death threat brought some urgency to address all of that. He was her biggest fan and made sure he met all her needs, no matter how taxing things were at times.

Theresa and I went to the appointment the next day. Margaret was at work. I think that was a saving grace. I knew this appointment was going to be like no other. Theresa had something on her mind and wanted to share it with him, or perhaps just tell him, "Thank you."

I told her I could wait outside so she could talk to him privately. She insisted I come in. "I need you to help me through this." We waited in the room for some time. Dr. Reeves was usually punctual, but today, we had to wait for a long time, making her that much more anxious.

As we sat, she said to me, "How do I ask him? How do I say this? How do I let go to die?"

When he came in, he was dressed in a suit. He smiled at both of us and greeted Theresa with a hug. I knew he could sense the heaviness in the room. He examined her. "Everything looks good. The drain site is a little red, but I don't think it's anything to be concerned about."

She nodded, not seeming to listen to what he was saying but rather focusing on what she wanted to talk about. He got a telephone call and stepped out of the room for a moment.

I could see she was uneasy. "Just tell him what's on your mind," I insisted.

He came back in the room and began discussing the recent pelvic pain she had been experiencing. She was anxious to talk, but let him finish his statement.

"Okay, forget that for a minute," she said. "I'm done."

He asked for clarification. "Done? What are you done with? I hope you don't think I've been forcing you to continue treatment."

She rushed to get the words out before beginning to cry. "No, just the opposite. I have had you running through hoops to keep me here, and now I'm finished. I'm tired, and the pain is beyond bearable. I just don't know how I go about letting go."

We had come to know him very well, and he always seemed to get a certain frown when he was concerned or upset.

He swallowed hard and rolled his chair closer to her. "You just up the pain meds, and let yourself go through the process, out of pain and resting. I'm confident you'll get in a few dances at your daughter's wedding. But then, you need to focus on yourself."

"I've barely been eating, and I really don't care to." She pointed to me. "It upsets her."

I looked over at him and tried to speak without crying. "In the beginning, it was one thing, but now I have to let her do what she feels she wants to do. I'm not going to force her to eat."

"Everyone knows it's getting close, and they understand you need to let go," he proclaimed.

For the first time, I couldn't hold back my tears. I felt bad for him, two crying girls in his office. It was remarkable how he could hold it together. I tried not to speak much. I knew I probably wouldn't get but a few words out without sobbing.

She thanked him as we left the exam room. He walked to his office, not looking back at us. "I want to see those wedding pictures," he said. I knew in my heart he was upset and gathered all the energy he had inside not to show it.

We waited in the hall for the elevator. I gained my composure, and Theresa gave me a big hug. "I'm glad Margaret wasn't here. I would have never made it through the appointment. Don't tell her all this. I don't want to upset her."

When we got back to the house, I jumped in the shower to settle my nerves from the emotional day. When I came out, we each took a couch and played on our phones. No words shared between us, but we were sharing time together like kids.

She said, "I feel like we're waiting for Mom and Dad to come home."

We both laughed.

When we got back home, Carly came to check on Theresa and possibly up her medications. What once took the edge off now barely helped her get through even a few hours without excruciating pain. The new dose seemed to allow her not to be so anxious. She seemed much more settled. Seemingly, she was more tired, but didn't seem to fight the feeling anymore.

"The sun feels so good coming through the window; it's so relaxing," she said. "It just feels so amazing."

She was barely tube feeding now, and her mood toward the outside world was changing. Her days just seemed to run together. I walked Carly to her car, and we spoke at length about what was to come. Visibly shaken, Theresa's decline affected Carly, too. People don't realize it affects the doctors and nurses as well. Getting close to a patient was an occupational hazard. She told me cancer and the medications combined were making Theresa seem distant. The fact that she was much calmer was the most important thing right now.

Theresa's bursts of energy seemed few and far between now, and most times only driven by last-minute details of Veronica's wedding or her anticipation to see Christopher when he came home.

"I hope he gets what is happening," she claimed. "I worry when I'm gone. It's going to hit him really hard."

I told her he got it, but nothing will make the sadness any easier, nor could she control what lay ahead.

The wedding next week was quickly approaching. Scheduled the weekend of Thanksgiving, Theresa feared the attendance would be low because of the holiday, but, gladly, that was not the case. She didn't want her health to overshadow the wedding, but I knew a lot of people were coming to say their last farewells.

Christopher arrived home, and I knew deep in Theresa's heart, she was just glad she got to see him one more time. She insisted on going with Derek and Christopher for the last-minute tuxedo alterations. I pulled Christopher aside and told him to hold onto her. She was extremely weak, and I didn't want her falling. Besides all the commotion surrounding the event, Theresa seemed so peaceful, I was not sure if it was the drugs or a higher power giving her comfort.

When they arrived back at the house, Theresa was spent. Not another ounce of fuel was left inside her. Christopher gently helped his mom up the stairs and kissed her on the forehead. When I glanced in the bedroom, she was lying flat on the bed, staring up at the ceiling. Her eyelids were so dark, I thought she was wearing eyeshadow. Each time I looked at her, I wished for her to go in peace, but then found myself selfishly asking for just one more day. I was tired and on my last nerve. Not in a bad way. I just felt like I was running the course with her; united into one soul, and I, too, was running out of fuel.

The wedding day was finally upon us. Theresa could no longer stand for any length of time, so I had her lie on the bed to put on her makeup. A big grin came over her face while I was carefully trying to put on her mascara.

"Hold still or you are going to look like Joan Crawford," I insisted.

"I made it," she declared. "I really made it."

She looked amazing in a one-shoulder beaded gown. Christopher walked his mom down the aisle. She glided gracefully through the aisle of flowers while holding on tightly. The ceremony was beautiful, and she mouthed to me "Thank you," as the wedding couple recited their vows.

As the night forged on, she lay down in a private room and only came into the banquet hall for the first dance and cutting of the cake. Theresa was happy she could give her daughter this special day. She stood on the dance floor holding tightly to Mom and Dad, and then spoke with friends the best she could. The looks on their faces were more than I could bear. The pain that each of her closest friends tried to hide was heartbreaking. She pretended not to notice, but knew all the while this was the last time she would see most of them. I stayed where she could see me, in case she needed me to escort her back to lie down. She was so cold to the touch. I put her sweatpants on underneath her gown and gave her a jacket to keep her warm while laying her back down on the makeshift bed.

None of that seemed to help as she shivered intensely. Veronica came in a short time later, kneeling to give her mom a big hug and a kiss on the cheek. She glanced up at me when she felt the frigid touch on her mother's face.

"I think I need to take her home," I remarked.

Veronica nodded in agreement, and we helped her sit up. "Love you, Mom. You made this such an amazing day for me."

The whole drive home, Theresa leaned her head against the glass. We held hands in silence. I cranked up the heater to try to warm her. Beads of sweat began to form on my face from the blasting heat, but she continued to tremble.

Once back home, I helped take off her dress and wig and bundled her up in a robe and her favorite beanie like a newborn. This became our evening ritual as her body temperature dropped more and more frequently. Her delicate frame finally began to settle from the shivering; the medications had kicked in, and she was finally peaceful. I zipped her dress and shoes in a garment bag and methodically organized her blankets. Neither of us said much. She was so happy, and I felt fortunate to have helped her make it this far.

I wheeled her feeding pole closer to the bed and began to prepare the feeding bag, but she turned her face toward me and waved me off that she wasn't doing that tonight. I worried her room was now becoming more like a hospital room than the once-welcoming suite I had designed for her. At that moment, I realized, with tremendous regret, it was becoming just that.

She smiled at me. I leaned over and gave her a lengthy hug. I'll remember that moment always because it felt so final. When I pulled back from her, she gleamed with a quietness and immense peace. "Thank you for helping me stay true to myself." She let out a long exhale. "You have helped me find my way back to who I am. I love you."

I grinned at her and said, "Good night," trying not to break down right there in front of her. "Get some rest," I ordered. "Good stuff tomorrow."

I closed her door quietly behind me, and then went into the backyard in a hidden corner and tried to stop myself from bawling hysterically. When I finally got to bed, Matt and I spoke briefly about the wedding. I must have fallen asleep while we were talking because the next thing I saw was Theresa standing at the foot of our bed. Startled, I blinked my eyes a few times to see if I was dreaming. Riley stood and flapped his ears, so I knew I wasn't hallucinating.

"You okay?" I sat up in bed.

"I think I forgot to take my pills," she claimed.

I rolled myself off the bed and walked over to her. "I have my alarm set to give you your medication," I told her. "You don't need to keep track."

I put my arm around her and walked her back to her room. Her increased medication and lack of focus had me concerned for her safety. She insisted on getting out of bed at night. I was worried that, in her fragile condition, she would fall and hurt herself. The last thing I wanted was to have her spend her last days in a hospital. I blew up an air mattress and slept next to her bed. Out of exhaustion, I would fall asleep, yet in the middle of the night, I would awake to her foot stepping on me. When I would tell her to wake me, she would just give me a smirk.

So, I set a motion detector to aid me in keeping an eye on her. But, that, too, proved to be a comedy of errors. I found her many times trying to dismantle the device with her foot without setting it off. The funny thing was that she had the foresight to dismantle the alarm, but not wake me if she needed to get up.

"How do I get this thing not to ding?" she inquired. "It's annoying."

I couldn't help but laugh. "You want to know how to keep it from dinging Stop trying to get out of bed without waking me."

We shared a room growing up, and here we were once again. We laughed and cried, but mostly laughed. I would lie on the floor next to her bed and try to imagine we were kids again, and her leaving me soon was all just a horrible dream.

One of the nights amongst the laughter, she stopped abruptly and said, "You know, this has been the best year of my life." Seemed almost crazy to believe someone could say that from all the suffering she endured. I knew what she meant, and ironically, it was the best year for me as well.

She had allowed me to find myself once again. I, for the first time, had a purpose, a purpose that wasn't about driving myself into the ground to please others and to make their lives easier at the expense of my own well-being. Keeping her alive had meaning and value. I was no longer putting myself at risk of self-destruction, but rather picking my battles, and fighting for the ones that had the most significance.

The truth is, we all try to give our lives meaning, but along the way, we tend to get lost in those things that are not important. We suffocate ourselves with trying to do right by others, while harming our innermost personal self in the process. I was that person, but no longer. I was given a gift; I promised myself not to squander the life lesson I had learned at the expense of losing her. A life would be lost to give me this wisdom, and that held tremendous value.

Chapter 16

She used to go with me when I walked Riley. I would bundle her up so as not to catch a cold. She enjoyed sitting in the car, playing games on her phone while Riley and I made the brisk walk around the park. She just didn't seem trustworthy anymore. Her mind was slipping. My biggest fear was I would come back to the car, and she would be gone.

That Sunday morning, Matt took Riley to play at his favorite park. The last few days Riley seemed a bit out of sorts, spending more and more time at the foot of Theresa's bed. The chance to run and play with his dog friends seemed like a welcome change.

When Matt returned, I heard him calling my name from downstairs. The concern in his voice was obvious. I rushed down the stairs to find him hugging Riley. He looked up at me with tears in his eyes.

"He's blind," he claimed. "I don't think he can see anything."

I stood, looking at them, wondering if he had gotten hurt or something. There were no signs of injury, just Matt's continued claims.

"What happened?"

Riley stood still, while Matt checked him over. He was visibly nervous. Matt made gestures to see if he could see anything. As he tried to walk, he bumped into anything that was in his path, circling, and then finally lying down out of exhaustion and fear.

"I threw the ball to him in the field," he explained. "I told him to get it, and he just stood still, confused, in the middle of the grass. I thought he was just being stubborn, but as I walked toward him, I realized something was wrong. He sat down in the grass and waited for me to reach him."

In all the commotion, I didn't realize Theresa was standing behind me. She was so distraught. I could barely calm her down. She was more upset about Riley's condition than she had ever been about her own. Riley sensed her pain, got up and walked toward her.

"He's coming with me, isn't he?" she blurted out.

Riley was my baby, and that was the *last* thing I needed to hear. I sat down on the floor next to him, trying to comfort him. As I stroked his back, he was motionless. I wrapped my arms around him, giving him a long hug, as his eyes remained closed.

Matt called our local veterinarian, who insisted we bring Riley right over. We all piled into the car. I was concerned about bringing Theresa along in her weak condition, but she insisted and I couldn't leave her home alone.

The veterinarian examined him, and then, without hesitation, said, "He's blind for sure. It's SARDS."

We all sat stunned, as he acted as if this was business as usual. He explained it could happen to dogs unexpectedly, yet most could go on to live a normal life with some minor adjustments. He used the analogy of when a pet loses a leg, it adjusted. I found it hard to believe that a young, healthy dog could go blind without complications or warning. Yet, apparently, SARDS is just that . . . Sudden Acquired Retinal Degeneration Syndrome.

We went home in disbelief, but willing to do whatever we needed to do to help him adjust. Theresa sat on the couch, hugging Riley. The confusion on his face was apparent. Matt jumped on the computer, researching and ordering supplies to help Riley with his transition. During his search, he found an ophthalmologist for dogs.

Meanwhile, I fought to keep myself from caving into yet another heart-wrenching blow. My relationship with Riley was more than dog and owner. Our time together had such deep meaning. On many occasions, our walks became counseling sessions for me. He was my therapist, my spiritual advisor. He gave me time to clear my head and gain strength from his love and devotion. Losing him, too, would be more than I think my heart could bear.

Our focus turned to Riley the next morning. I had Sophie come over to stay with Theresa while we went to the animal eye doctor. After lengthy testing, the doctor determined it wasn't his eyes; his eyes were healthy. Not only wasn't it his eyes, he said it was not SARDS either. "It's something in his brain," he said with caution. "I have a neurologist I want you to see."

Matt and I were beside ourselves. I hugged Riley, while Matt made the appointment with the neurologist. I was so angry and disgusted that our veterinarian we trusted had brushed it off with such conviction.

Riley was the thread that had been holding together this fragile passage for me with Theresa. I know it sounds crazy, but he didn't judge, he didn't have opinions; he only had unconditional love that was getting me through the toughest thing I had to face in my entire life. Like Theresa, he was too young, too vibrant, to be taken away so easily.

I think something dramatic occasionally happens in your life to knock you off course and change the road on which you are traveling. Theresa had changed my life in so many ways. Why now was I being given *another* test? Something else that would change me again? I felt like a pinball bouncing around from emotion to emotion.

In the morning, we took a long drive to the neurologist's office. After some lengthy testing, she determined he had encephalitis, an autoimmune disease, which was mounting an attack against his brain. She opted to keep him for a few days and began to barrage his system with cyclosporine, a chemotherapy pill to aid in suppressing the overactive immune attack. We remained optimistically guarded, but felt Riley was in good hands.

In her declining condition, I feared this would push her right over the edge. I forced myself to lie to her, reassuring her that he would be fine when he returned home.

Night after night, she sobbed in her room. She held a vigil for him until he returned. "We need to do the white sage in the house and get rid of the bad mojo," she insisted, "before he comes home." The negative energy in the house was overwhelmingly evident, and she wanted it gone.

When we brought Riley home, his eyesight seemed to return rather quickly. However, the drugs he was on made him very sick. The doctor assured us this was the best course of treatment, to just hang in there and keep him comfortable. This was like watching Theresa go through her one and only chemotherapy session that almost killed her.

Over the next few weeks, Theresa would get markedly worse. She stopped answering her phone most days, and although I tried to explain to everyone that she was sleeping a lot, no one seemed to get it. Derek was oblivious, insisting it was a phone malfunction rather than her condition.

At one time, she was worried about him and trusted he would stop relying on her for everything, hoping he would gain strength like her children had done through the process, realizing she would soon be gone. But, he didn't, and she finally came to terms with the fact that she couldn't do any more for him, comfortable that she prepared him the best she could.

Carly had given me a book about the stages of death as Theresa began to decline. When I initially read it, I figured this was just a blanket guide to living with a dying person. However, as the weeks before her death unfolded, each step in the book were spot-on accurate. As her condition progressed, she slept more and more, distancing herself from most of the outside world other than Riley and me. Theresa loved Riley, and he loved her. Every night he would go into her room. She would hang her head off the bed, and he would give her a big kiss. They were joined. He knew she needed him, and he would put his well-being aside to comfort her.

As Christmas was fast approaching, I couldn't help but remember those profound words from her doctor. "If she makes it to Christmas, it'll be a gift."

Somehow, I judged everything by that time frame, especially as she got blatantly weaker. I asked her if she had made a Christmas list.

"You told me asking for organs is not an option, right?" She chuckled.

I prayed now each day that God took her. It was time, and I didn't want her to suffer anymore. I saw her stare at herself in the mirror and wondered whose protruding frame of bones was looking back at her. Her other self was gone, leaving her with an unrecognizable figure in the reflection. I knew it still bothered her even at this level.

Her feeding tube seemed to have a mind of its own, constantly trying to escape. She insisted we go see Doctor Reeves, claiming it was for the feeding tube, but in my heart, I knew she just wanted to see him one last time.

Matt assured me Riley would be fine while we were gone and encouraged me to get on the road early before traffic. Although torn between Riley and my sister, I needed to help her finalize each remaining task.

Doctor Reeves gave her a big hug when we arrived and asked to see the wedding photos; he sat close to her, looking at the pictures. "I never got to swim with the sea turtles in Hawaii, but I made my daughter really happy." She beamed. "I was strung out on such a stressful existence until this last year; I finally gave myself that great big amazing life I've always hoped for."

Doctor Reeves fixed her feeding tube in the outpatient surgery suite and showed the nurses the wedding photos while she rested on the gurney. As we went to leave, she leaned into his body and gave him a hug. "Thank you again for everything," she said quietly.

He smiled without uttering a word. I tucked her tiny body under my arm, and we walked out the double doors. As we turned the corner almost out of sight, she looked over her shoulder and smiled at him one more time.

"He sure made dying easy," she claimed. "I'll never forget him."

As we left Margaret's house in the morning, she waved to us from the front stoop. I could see her in my rearview mirror, wiping the tears from her eyes. Our memories of laughter and tears at our home away from home would be with us forever. We spent some of the best and worst times behind those walls; times we would always treasure and never forget.

On the drive home, Theresa told me she wished she could go on a date with a smoking hot guy. "I want a twelve," she insisted, "like in the romance novels."

We laughed and I told her maybe I should call one of those last wish groups to arrange it. Even at this juncture, she still made each day something to remember. I wish I had her nerve; she had so much courage. She didn't spend any days fearing the worst, but rather focusing on the best.

Phyllis called and wanted to stop by when she got off work. She would have the formidable task of handling

Theresa's estate when she was gone and insisted on making sure she understood each wish. However, Theresa didn't want to hear it anymore. She had laid it out as clear as she could and knew Phyllis could handle any loose ends. Her children would be well taken care of. No more planning was necessary.

Everyone had a different way of handing Theresa's illness. Sophie chose not to come around much, pretending that if she ignored her sister's fate, it would somehow go away, which was how she handled most things in her life, so it didn't seem odd she would do the same in this instance. I finally had to have a come-to-Jesus conversation with her. I knew if she didn't spend more time with her sister, she would regret it; she needed to put on her big-girl panties and face the harsh reality of life. As we all dreaded the day when she would be gone, as hard to accept as it was, it *was* going to happen.

Over this past year, Phyllis came almost every night after work to spend time with Theresa. She was a biology teacher who took her job and most situations very seriously. Very strong willed, she doesn't let emotions get in the way of the right decision. Perhaps that's why Theresa chose her to handle her affairs. Yet, somehow, her sister's condition softened her, for the better, I think. The pain on her face when she left my house each night made me truly realize the barriers were down, and she would never allow herself to be as vulnerable as she was during this time.

James had fallen on some hard times, so he had been living with us throughout this passage. Yet, he felt uncomfortable about going into her room, so the times he spent with her were only when Theresa was downstairs. Growing up with five sisters, somehow, he felt he couldn't invade her privacy. He shaped his actions around this false injunction that he could not cross those boundaries without consent. Respecting her privacy was one thing, but he took it to an all-new level. He called Theresa the United Nations of the family, always willing to take the blame when we were kids, so the others could avoid punishment. She never took sides, but she helped us glue ourselves back together when times were tough.

James had been in some dark places himself a few times, escaping death from a robbery at his work when he was in his thirties. He seemed the most in touch with facing death; the balance of his life seemed to have hovered just above a catastrophic event. He never seemed to be able to get himself back on his feet; perhaps that's why he looked up to Theresa. He watched her when she seemed to have run out of options to pick herself up, and try to survive what was in front of her rather than accept her fate without a fight.

As kids, Margaret was the mother of the siblings. Being the oldest girl, she protected us and helped each of us through tough times we didn't think we could talk to Mom and Dad about or handle on our own. I think deep down, she felt a tremendous guilt for not being able to fix this for her little sister. Theresa stayed so strong with all of us, facing this fast-moving train without any hint of weakness. I'm not sure how she did it. I think Margaret knew Theresa was an integral link in our family and once she was gone, would we all stay as close as we had become? I know the sadness for her was like a giant wave she couldn't swim through, thinking she would wash away in the whitewater once Theresa was gone.

She and I had become so close, but I, too, worried once Theresa was gone the funny stories we shared would be overshadowed and deteriorate from the sadness. Many a night at her house, the three of us were hysterical with laughter at the stories no one else would ever think were funny or were too morbid to try to see the upside.

My deepest regret would be the minutes, hours, and days that would be void of her wit. There would soon come a time when we were no longer all present and accounted for, and it made me dread each second knocked off the clock that brought me closer to her leaving.

Once again, that evening, I lay on the air mattress below her. I have been staying on a schedule with her medication, trying to keep her calm and out of so much pain. Her breathing more labored, she struggled to swallow even the smallest pill. Carly showed me how to crush the pills in a spoon, add water, and then, using a syringe, slowly administer it in her mouth. This would be my only option now, since she was unable to swallow.

We spoke about the past, and she shared some deep, personal stories she had never revealed to anyone. I assured her when she was gone her most personal possessions would stay with me. Now was not going to be the time to delete old e-mails or clean her computer from her private life. Her thoughts needed to remain her thoughts, and when she was gone, those things she chose to keep to herself would remain there forever.

Theresa thrived on being strong for everyone in her life. She wanted to make sure there wouldn't be pandemonium when she was finally gone. She insisted on talking about her funeral arrangements, which I skirted around the conversation most days, but she was persistent.

I finally said, "This is like planning your own surprise party. I know what you want; no funeral parlor atmosphere." I smiled. "I'll make sure there will be drinks flowing and plenty of laughs, with a splash of mischief, just like you."

Over the next week or so, my time with her was getting shorter and shorter. Her sleeping had become more and more

215

frequent with longer durations of unconsciousness. When she was awake, she was very tranquil and her response to questions had become very sluggish. I knew she understood me, but she processed her reply much slower and with very few words. Her eyes changed from the bright ocean-blue color to a dull grey. She completely stopped feeding and only drank small sips of water. Her weight was lower than I thought anyone's body could endure.

"I thank God for a wonderful life. Two amazing kids and a family anyone would love to be a part of. I don't get to pick when I leave . . . So, I don't know why I feel it is coming, just a sense. I have talked to almost everyone I need to. It's weird . . . It's not so much the pain as it is the feeling of emptiness. . . nothing left. It has nothing to do with those I love or fighting to be with them. That I will do until my last breath. It's a pull to have peace, to not wonder . . . to not be afraid."

— From Theresa's Journal

It was Christmas Eve. I stroked Theresa's shoulder lightly to wake her. I wanted to change her bandages and administer her medication. I realized her feeding tube had detached somehow and was flapping loosely against her abdomen. She lay in bed, semi-alert, as I cleaned her stomach and coiled up the tube, taping it down to her skin. Even though she hadn't used it in weeks, I didn't want to alarm her about its escape. I think it was somehow a security blanket for her, perhaps a lifeline.

Mom insisted we keep the family tradition and go to a local Italian restaurant with the whole family. I told her I didn't think Theresa would be able to handle the outing, but she was persistent. I had offered for the whole family to come to my house, but she wasn't having it.

"This is a tradition," she insisted. "We're going to the restaurant."

It seemed selfish at the rawest level, but perhaps this was a way for her to cope with her forever-changing family. When we got to the restaurant, everyone had already arrived. I held Theresa's arm and escorted her to the head of the table next to Dad. By the look on everyone's faces, the family seemed

truly shocked by Theresa's appearance. Usually, she was in a nightgown or covered up with a sweater and her beanie. Tonight, she was dressed in a cute outfit that her bony body was barely able to feel the fabric against her skin. She was so frail and struggled to keep her eyes focused on the people around her. We hardly stayed but a half hour and I had to take her home. My overprotective nature wanted to yell out, "Do you get it now?"

Once home, I changed her out of her clothes, laid her down, and bundled her up with a blanket. "They want us to come to Mom's after they're done at the restaurant," I told her. "But, we don't need to go."

She nodded. "Let's go."

I knew she was just doing it for the family. Her kids were there, and she wanted to keep that brave face, even though she was barely able to stand. Everyone mobbed her when we arrived. It felt somewhat like a freak show. She spent the rest of the evening lying on Mom's bed. Everyone took turns spending time with her, even though she was scarcely awake. I felt bad for being so overprotective, but any quality time should have been spent long before now. Precious time that passes is fragile and cannot be restored; once it's gone, it can never be regained. This, I think, was a harsh lesson to face for those who chose not to spend more time with her previously.

However, she did find tremendous comfort from Christopher's presence. Losing his mom would be an enormous blow for him, but he never pulled back from her out of fear. Each morning, he would call her from school, and I could hear her either laughing hysterically or trying to manage some event in his daily life. He was truly a young version of her—a tremendous sense of humor, with an unwavering loyalty and drive to be successful for himself and his mother. He truly made her proud, and I think her illness brought them that much closer to each other. No one could emulate his larger-than-life mother, but he is, undoubtedly, the product of her principles.

In the morning, I awoke to Theresa's foot stepping on my leg. It was early Christmas morning, and she was surprisingly awake and alert. I struggled to roll my body off the air mattress.

"Merry Christmas," I exclaimed. "Are you ready for presents?"

Riley had been keeping a vigilant watch over us throughout the evening. He arched his back and snapped his ears back and forth. Even though he was clearly not feeling good from the medication, his eyesight had fully returned, and he seemed to be doing much better.

I helped Theresa off the bed, and we headed downstairs to open presents. Matt got the video camera ready, and James helped with separating the gifts. I made a comfortable spot for Theresa on the couch and started handing her gift after gift. Christmas at our house has always been grand, and this year would be no different. With two of my siblings here to celebrate, it would be a holiday to remember.

Theresa looked over at me in shock as the presents kept piling up. Riley walked in and out of the numerous boxes, sniffing for his gifts. I sat close to Theresa, assisting in ripping through her presents. Her joy-filled reaction was the best gift I could have ever received. Tears rolled down her cheeks as she opened each present. All the surrounding noise got quiet in my head as I paused to take in the sight of it all. I tried to compress everything she might want in life into this last year. The crinkling of the wrapping paper and the twinkling Christmas tree lights in the background made me wish for this day to never end.

When all the commotion came to a halt, we stood in the center of the room, hugging each other. I tried so hard to hold it together, the well of tears lingered in my eyes until I could barely see across the room. Yet, I had one more gift that she would never expect. She had wanted a puppy for so long, one to cuddle with her and call her own.

I grabbed my purse and tried to sneak out undetected to pick up our new addition.

"Where are you going?" she insisted.

"I'll be right back," I claimed.

She pressured me further. "I'm coming with you."

I looked over at Matt for guidance. "Take her with you," he said. "She'll be fine."

Theresa glanced at Matt for some clue as to our adventure. "Do I need to pack a weapon?" she joked. "Come on, Riley, we might need backup." She chuckled.

As I pulled up to the town house where I would pick up her final gift, I felt a sense of peace. This was the gift she would never have expected, yet would be the one that would bring her so much happiness.

"I'll be right back," I insisted. "Give me a couple of minutes."

As I carried the teacup Yorkie in my arms, I could see her expression through the car glass. Her smile beamed as she rolled down the window in disbelief. She cried calmly and stretched her arms out to hold the puppy.

"She's mine? She's really mine?"

"Yep, here's your baby, Chloe."

My voice cracked as I watched the joy on her face. Riley sniffed his new baby sister, welcoming her into the family.

"He loves her, too," she babbled. "I can't believe this." Theresa loved *The Wizard of Oz*, and now she finally had her own Toto.

The New Year finally arrived, and like a time clock, Theresa began to decline quickly. My elderly parents came by for their daily afternoon visit. Theresa was usually sleeping so she didn't see them much anymore. My parents struggled to get upstairs, so most of their visits were merely their presence in the house. Mom sensed her daughter's death was nearing and decided she needed to make the trek upstairs. Theresa lay in her bed barely able to stay alert.

"Mom is going to come up and see you," I said.

She opened her eyes widely, swung her legs off the bed, and in one motion, grabbed me by the arm to help herself up. Without a word spoken, we made our way down the stairs. Even at that point, she remained concerned for those she loved. Her relationship with Mom was the strongest it had ever been or would ever be. When she emerged off the last step, Mom helped her down and held her as if she would never let her go.

Over the years, their relationship had some rocky times, but at that moment, I realized there is always comfort in your mother's arms. I could tell Theresa was keeping a brave face, but struggling to stay standing. I put her down on the couch and covered her with a blanket. She curled her legs under her nightgown to squash out the merciless pain. She would never make her way back upstairs after that day. She had become so weak and realized she willingly needed to confront her biggest fear: losing her independence.

That night, my husband and I moved her bed downstairs. That was probably one of the hardest things I have ever done. This was it. Her departure was coming soon, and I would be without her in the blink of an eye.

When she first came to stay with us, my goal was to give her some quality of life in her last months. I guess buried deep in my heart I thought I might somehow save her. Prior to now, she was adamant about staying in her own room upstairs. I told her it would be easier on her to stay in the downstairs room so she could reserve her energy, but it was as if she was giving into her illness. This time, however, she didn't fight it. The room that was once her safe haven would soon turn back into a guest room.

Matt set up the living room like a giant bedroom suite. He mounted a pole across the entrance where I hung a curtain to give her some privacy. I placed pictures of her kids in the windowsill next to her bed, so she could reach out and touch them. Family came and went, while most of the time she slept through the visits.

If she needed to get up for anything, one of us would assist her into the wheelchair and take her where she wanted to go. I would face her to lift her off the bed, wrapping her arms around my neck as I held her like a small child. When she was alert enough to sit up, she insisted on sitting on the edge of the bed, crossing her legs, and letting them dangle.

Before she stopped speaking, she made me promise that Christopher would return to school, no matter what happened. The afternoon prior to his departure, he and Veronica came by to spend some time with their mom. She would turn her head and smile at them sitting close to each other on the oversized couch. Christopher held his mother's hand and showed her pictures of his new track gear. She grinned with pride as she fell off to sleep once again.

I know neither of them wanted to make the decision to leave her side. I spoke with them quietly and assured them she was comfortable and out of pain. "She loves you both so much," I said. "You need to stay close. You are her whole life, and now you need to do the same for each other." They both struggled to stay strong, holding back the tears as they held hands leaving the house.

"They tell me when I'm right with God it will be okay. I wonder if that means God's not ready for me, or I'm not ready for Him. I think less of the future now. What makes me cry is knowing the kids' happy times will be somewhat overshadowed with sadness because they will think of me. I tried so hard to make our lives so full of laughter and joy. This is the hard part, knowing I will cause them pain. They will be okay in the end, and I will be watching and smiling."

— From Theresa's Journal

Carly had arranged to have someone come to the house to bathe Theresa. A young girl appeared at my front door, carrying a duffle bag. She introduced herself and asked if there were any requests. "Nope. I'll give her some privacy. Call me if you need anything."

I pulled the curtain closed behind me, went to the kitchen to light Theresa's favorite candle so she could smell the aroma. It was serene in the house; the only sound was the splashing water as the aide wrung out the washcloth. When she finished, Theresa looked so calm and peaceful. I escorted the young woman to the front door. She reached out and shook my hand.

"I'll see you again soon," she claimed. I knew she was only being cordial, but her calm, gentle nature gave Theresa that much more serenity.

I was both mentally and physically exhausted. Matt stayed by her side that night so I could get some rest. I lay on the air mattress just out of sight. He turned the television on low, and I could hear him talking to Theresa about the movie.

The next day was a gorgeous winter morning. The air was crisp, and white, fluffy clouds hung high above the house, while the turtledoves sat perched on the wall in plain view. Matt went upstairs to get some rest, and I sat by Theresa's side, talking to her. Her eyes remained closed, but she would grin periodically at things I would say to her. Her breathing was shallow; she took short bursts of air, and then seemingly held her breath for long stretches in between.

I knew today was going to be the day. It was only a matter of time. I phoned no one about her failing condition. I held to her wishes that it just be she and I at the end. I glanced at the clock. It was 1:45 p.m. I stroked her hand and continued to talk to her; she remained motionless.

Riley insisted on getting on the bed next to her. He usually stayed on the floor as her protector, but, today, he gently jumped up on the bed and laid his entire body pressed up against hers. His cheeks puffed up with air, and then he let out a long exhale. She draped her arm across his back; they were both still with their eyes closed. I knew he felt her time with us was ending, and he wanted her to know he would forever be by her side.

"Christopher is in the air now," I proclaimed. "He's on his way back to school."

In those short minutes following, she never moved. Her body seemed completely relaxed.

"I love you," I told her. "We will see each other soon."

With those last few words uttered, she opened her eyes wide, staring up at the corner of the room. She smiled, and then gently closed her eyes again. I leaned down and lay my head on her chest for that last glimmer of life . . . and then she was gone.

She had forever changed my life, and nothing can take that from me. My days are filled with sadness, some better than others. I continue to think I will hear her voice or see her, but those moments have passed. I hope she will keep her promise and leave her fingerprint impression on my walls so I will know she's still with me.

She lived these last months with true meaning and took her last breath knowing everyone loved her. She always said she was just a visitor on this great earth, and it was her time to go home. I became a different person through it all; yet, a piece of me died with her as well. I wish for those moments when my mind gives me a break, allowing me to feel whole again. In most families, ours included, you may not always like each other, but you will always love each other. Appreciate the family you have and hold them tight. Live each day with what is true in your heart. Those times you let pass . . . never come around again.

CPSIA information can be obtained
at www.ICGtesting.com
Printed in the USA
LVHW09*1334011018
592005LV00007B/46/P